HOME COOKED

WITHDRAWN

Essential
recipes for
a new way
to cook

HOME COOKED

ANYA FERNALD

Belcampo Founder and CEO
with Jessica Battilana

Photography by Brown W. Cannon III

TEN SPEED PRESS
Berkeley

This book is dedicated to Anne & Russ Fernald

WELCOME

TAKE A SEAT

STAY A WHILE

My kitchen: an introduction

Today, having your child choose a career in farming has become almost prestigious, as America's interest in food has reached new heights. But I assure you that back in 1993, when I graduated high school, no one in Palo Alto, California, was dreaming their daughter would grow up to run a meat company. My parents had been charmed by my entrepreneurial spunk when I started a cookie business as a teen and were happy that I was able to cook for them from a fairly young age, but when I announced my plans they were worried about what exactly I would end up *doing*.

My parents are academics and school is pretty important to them. I went to college mostly to make them happy, but even then I knew my career was going to have a culinary bent. I got a fellowship straight out of college that provided me with the funds to spend a year working in cheese dairies in very rural parts of southern Europe and northern Africa. To get around on the cheap, I bought a folding bicycle and figured out how to use the train system. My budget for the whole year of travel was $25,000: $20,000 from the fellowship and a $5,000 check my grandfather gave me as my college graduation present. The fellowship was for recent college graduates to "expand their horizons" in a field where there was no linear path to further their expertise, and artisan cheese making certainly checked that box.

Most days I woke at the crack of dawn and cycled down some bumpy road to visit a dairy, trying to get there when the milk was still warm. I visited the United Kingdom, Switzerland, France, Greece, Tunisia, and Italy, stopping in at farms and dairies all along the way. I learned a lot about self-reliance in that year, even spent a night in a county jail in Greece (long story), but above all I learned to eat.

Every time I visited a dairy and spent a few hours hanging around the aging room with one of these rural masters, they would invariably invite me to join them for the main meal of the day, lunch. We would eat for a few hours and talk further, and I would see a meal unfold in traditional fashion: bread set right on the table, salt pinched out of a bowl (and it was different than the salt I was used to), butter spread thickly, and eggs or a big piece of fresh cheese drenched in oil as a main course.

At work at a sheep milk dairy in central Italy.

When I think back, a lot of the food I cook today came directly from what I learned from watching farmers eat simple food in their own homes. For example, I saw an animal being killed for the first time—a pig, in a courtyard, with a knife—and learned to make blood sausage and chicharróns that very same day.

I started that year of cheese making as a wannabe gourmet and ended it as a nascent farmer. I'd spent a year talking my way into dozens of dairies in languages I did not really speak and had developed a taste for travel and exploration. I was not ready to move back to the United States.

I had met a fairly well-organized research group—the Consorzio Ricerca Filiera Lattiero-Casearia (CoRFiLaC)—while I was visiting Sicily during my year of cheese making, and I was able to secure a work visa and a job offer from them. Shortly after, I moved to Ragusa, a town in southeastern Sicily, and began two years of work with a team that I affectionately nicknamed the Cheese Mob. At the time, the group was primarily responsible for managing denomination of origin labeling for cheese (these are the *DOP* or *AOC* labels you see on many quality European products), an authority that was taken from them in later years thanks to shady dealings.

When I worked there, the Cheese Mob was flush with EU cash, primarily earmarked for projects intended to stimulate the regional food economy in this underdeveloped region of Sicily. I led a business development program, and my work consisted of writing a few financial and marketing plans, attempting to implement them, organizing an export program, and eating a lot of epic dinners. In retrospect, the EU contracts must have stipulated that they hire someone who was not from Sicily, as I was definitely woefully underqualified for the job and can think of little reason that I would have landed it otherwise. But I remember feeling that I was in the right place when my first week of work landed me in a Sicilian village that was hosting a competition that involved rolling giant wheels of sheep's milk cheese down the mountainside in a sort of race (they boarded the windows and doors of the homes along the route—those cheeses moved fast).

As time went on, my work environment became increasingly operatic, with tears (regularly) and knives (occasionally) appearing during staff meetings, and my boss making the regular accusation that one or another of his core team were "betrayers." It was colorful and frankly pretty stressful for twenty-three-year-old me, but the life I was living made it worth it. I spent the weekends in the countryside, evenings in the piazza, ate granita with brioche for breakfast, and became fluent in Italian. I joined the town's marching band and played my oboe at all of the processions that marched through our town and the neighboring villages. The band's favorite piece to play while marching behind the swaying statue of the Virgin was the theme from *The Godfather*, which has an awesome oboe solo. I had fun.

One thing that really struck me was how the middle-class families in Ragusa were excited about eating at the new McDonald's in town. It was a status symbol to eat at this "see and be seen" place, since most of the cheese makers I worked with fed their families from their own small farms and by foraging in the surrounding forests. A meal at McDonald's meant your family had money to burn. Unlike in America, in Sicily, the poorer you were, the more likely you were to be eating organic, artisan-made foods. It was topsy-turvy: poor people had gardens, rich people were proud not to have gardens, and it was completely opposite to the emerging food scene in the States. Seeing that firsthand ignited a passion in me for social change around food, a passion that really came to life when I moved back home to California a few years later.

In Sicily, I learned how to find wild asparagus, how to crack open sea urchins, how to skin a warm pork belly fresh off the carcass. Depending on the season, poorer families in Ragusa would bake ricotta in the wood-fired oven to make it last through the winter or fill hundreds of empty beer bottles with fresh tomato pulp. For my friends there, these were skills they just grew up possessing and were eager to leave behind (so they could go eat at McDonald's). For me, a kid raised in the suburbs with easy access to a grocery store, this type of year-round "meal planning" was eye-opening. I had made jam with my mom before, but actually needing to put up a significant amount of food every month, all of it varying with the season, was a different level. There was also an ease of execution and a spontaneity that was impressive,

Left: Walking the cattle from high to low pastures in Sicily.

Right: Ragusano cheese in the aging room—the cheeses are hung from hemp ropes during aging.

something I later learned the Sicilians are famous for. I'd be chatting with my coworkers by the espresso machine close to lunchtime and someone would mention wanting to eat urchin now that the days were getting colder. Within a few minutes we'd have formed a plan, and within an hour, five of us would be in a little Zodiac boat with diving knives strapped to our legs, while one remained on shore to boil a big pot of water for the spaghetti and peel some garlic. Within the same hour, lunch was served on the rocks: *spaghetti ai ricci*. The Sicilians had a similar carefree attitude toward preserving the harvest. Faced with a glut of tomatoes or artichokes, they'd transform it, with little fanfare or planning, into something they'd eat all year-round. They all seemed to have a reserve of techniques that allowed them to quickly and spontaneously turn any abundant harvest into preserved food, something that deeply impressed and inspired me.

Some of my discoveries in Sicily were simple—like using a lot more fat than I was used to in cooking—or cooking only vegetables that were in season. But the true secret, if there was one, was preparing food using homemade or hyperlocal base ingredients, as most of the families I ate with did, from the fresh cheese in the lasagna to the home-dried herbs they mixed with salt and rubbed into meat.

After two years in Sicily, I moved to Piedmont to work at the headquarters of Slow Food International. The dysfunctional politics in Sicily had gotten to be a bit too much, and while I was not yet ready to leave Italy, I wanted a job with a more global impact. Slow Food was just that. It was a magical time for the organization: founded by the charismatic Carlo Petrini a decade earlier, it had just broken through internationally from its base in a small Piedmontese town (Alice Waters, Eric Schlosser, and Corby Kummer were regular faces in the headquarters in those early, heady days). When I joined, there were about forty of us on the payroll, one of whom was my future husband, Renato Sardo, who was the head of Slow Food International at the time. It was an incredible chapter in my life: we fell in love during a time of growth for a movement we both really believed in while living in Renato's hometown, which quickly felt like my hometown, too.

I started at Slow Food working on their English-language magazine and helping organize their international events. About six months into my tenure, Carlo Petrini decided to form the Slow Food Foundation as a means of concretely supporting farmers and food makers. I started working at that foundation directing microloans and investments that helped small-scale food producers around the globe grow production and comply with food safety laws. I think back on this period in my career as an on-the-ground MBA in small food and farm businesses. I worked with a group of women from Bosnia to help export their delicate plum preserves and with air-dried reindeer bresaola makers in Sweden's Sami region to bring their product up to code for EU distribution. Part of the mission of my company, Belcampo, is to "balance traditional food production techniques with economic viability," a philosophy that comes directly from this time in my life, when I saw how small farms were struggling to make ends meet. I saw how challenging it was to make something delicious, with integrity, and make money doing it. After six years of living in Italy, I missed home, and Renato and I, at that time married, decided to return to California.

It was only when we moved back that I realized how much I had changed. I had previously had a flash of how different I had become when I saw my sister's face, aghast at the massive platters of *carne cruda* and raw pork sausage we served at our wedding on a hot sunny day in Italy, and hadn't really understood why she thought that was weird. But Stateside, the difference became more pronounced. I had left the United States a child of the low-fat 1980s and '90s and returned with a hunger for salami and butter sandwiches, and my cooking style had developed a distinctly old-world sensibility and cadence.

Within six months of moving back to California, I bought a cow. A dead one. I wanted good beef at a reasonable price, and I also wanted braising cuts that I couldn't find at the store. I coordinated the purchase with a few friends but still was blindsided by the total volume of meat. I ended up strapping the freezer in my tiny apartment in Oakland, California, closed with electrical tape and baking dozens of meat loaves out of my mountain of ground beef. I also started buying a whole pig every year to process into salami and cured meats, vacuum-packing a few months' worth of sausages for my freezer.

Inside the Belcampo slaughterhouse where we age our beef carcases.

My career continued in a way that, in retrospect, feels linear: I started a produce-distribution business with very small California farms and ran a farm-to-school program, then returned briefly to the Slow Food fold when Alice Waters asked me to orchestrate a massive event in San Francisco—Slow Food Nation—that involved, among other things, planting a half-acre vegetable garden in front of San Francisco's city hall. On the tail of that event's success, I was able to launch my own consulting business doing the type of work I had done for the Slow Food Foundation investees. I developed business plans for a dozen or so clients, including Todd Robinson, a veteran of the financial world who wanted to invest in the sustainable food world. Within months of meeting Todd, we had begun work on an idea that would bring a new scale and ambition to a high-quality artisan food business.

We founded Belcampo together in 2011 and I had the opportunity of a lifetime—a chance to work on a bigger venture than anything I had ever tackled before. With Todd's backing and commitment, we started building a vertically integrated supply chain for pasture-raised organic meat. I bought land to build our slaughterhouse near our California farm at the end of 2011, and in 2012 my team was able to build the first multispecies slaughterhouse certified by the USDA in the state in decades. Shortly after, we opened our first butcher shop and restaurant, and since then our team has opened eight more locations. In the meantime, our company took over a property Todd had purchased in Belize, revamping the restaurant, renovating the existing hotel, and planting hundreds of acres of cacao, sugarcane, and other tropical

Left: My little girl Viola eating a lamb chop.

Right: Grilling at the farm.

crops. Our growth at Belcampo has been in step with a new interest in sustainable, quality food that is produced with techniques that go beyond organic certification: careful management of pasture and ecosystem, humane animal handling, and artisanal processing techniques.

Belcampo has given me many things, but chief among them was the farm that I had longed for since leaving Italy. I go to the farm—near Mount Shasta, close to the Oregon border—as often as I can, where I cook with our team and my friends, and where my toddler daughter loves to join me for all sorts of adventures, including lots of grilling (free access to a lawn with a goat chop in hand is her happy place). Being close to the ingredients we raise and the easy access to a lot of wood and a few big grills inspire me. I also get down to our farm in Belize every three or four months, where we have a huge organic vegetable garden to feed guests at our hotel.

Throughout my journey, from cheese maker on a folding bicycle to CEO of a sustainable agriculture company, I've tried to take an old-world approach to food and craftsmanship and make it relevant to modern American life. Belcampo and the nonprofit Food Craft Institute, which I started in Oakland to teach business skills and food safety to new food businesses, are a few of the ways I've tried to share my approach with others. But much of it is more personal—I hope to inspire friends to celebrate traditional recipes and the ritual of breaking bread together by cooking dinners, hosting canning parties, and creating celebrations around food. I am fortunate that my life's work and passion align deeply. Through the recipes in this book, I've tried to capture the core of the food of my life, the food that taught me about the pleasure of cooking, and the food I make now to share that pleasure with others.

Enjoy,

Anya Fernald

BUILDING BLOCKS

Many of us have had that experience when traveling of tasting some simple dish that we've had a million times before and wondering how the heck it tastes so much better than the version we've always eaten. I think that the answer to that question, the vast majority of the time, is that the base ingredients are often homemade and simply of a higher quality.

During my years in Italy, I spent a lot of my time cooking and eating with families. I was struck by how quickly and easily those home cooks were able to create meals that had extraordinary depth of flavor, something I'd typically come to associate with long cooking and fussy recipes. What I learned was how Italian cooks instead relied on "longcuts"—that is, the time-consuming base ingredients they made when time and ingredients were abundant, then preserved to use when they weren't. I think of this approach as a throwback to the way our grandparents cooked, when people spent time throughout the year putting up base ingredients to be used later.

In rural Italy, I rarely encountered store-bought building blocks, or pantry staples. Whether it was canned tomatoes, creamy rendered lard, or dried herbs, they were all homemade, then used to enhance fast dishes like pasta with tomato sauce or fried eggs with vegetables.

Inspired by what I learned in Italy, I now spend energy on the preparation of a few base ingredients. They are culinary crutches of the very best kind, and though it may seem counterintuitive, investing a chunk of time up front to stock my pantry and freezer actually allows me to prepare great food quickly, simply, and easily.

SOFRITTO

MAKES ABOUT 4 CUPS

Many recipes begin with first cooking down a mixture of onions, celery, and carrots until sweet and caramelized, forming the foundation of a dish. It's not complicated, but it is time-consuming. As a timesaver, I make a large batch of sofritto all at once, then freeze it in ice cube trays. Once frozen, I store the cubes in a plastic freezer bag, adding them as needed to braises, soups, ragu, and dozens of other dishes as a way of quickly adding long-cooked flavor to a dish.

| 1 cup extra-virgin olive oil | 4 large carrots, peeled and coarsely diced |
| 4 large white onions, coarsely diced | 4 celery stalks, coarsely diced |

In a large heavy frying pan, heat the olive oil over low heat. Add the onions, carrots, and celery and cook, stirring occasionally, until the vegetables have softened and caramelized, about 1½ hours. Let cool, then transfer to the bowl of a food processor and process until smooth.

Spoon the sofritto into ice cube trays and freeze. Once frozen, transfer the cubes to a plastic freezer storage bag. Keep in the freezer until ready to use; the sofritto will keep, frozen, for up to 6 months.

RECIPES USING SOFRITTO
Eggs Poached in Tomato (page 118), Beef & Pork Ragu (page 128), Bird & Bunny Ragu (page 132), Squash & Farro Risotto (page 133), Fresh Tomato Risotto (page 134), Stuffed Zucchini Blossoms in Tomato Sauce (page 138), Trotter Beans (page 165), Squid & Beans (page 190), Braised Tripe (page 192), Beer-Braised Rabbit with Shallots (page 208)

AIOLI

MAKES ABOUT 1 CUP

Homemade aioli provides a lot of bang for your buck—it's a versatile, righteously delicious condiment. It can be gussied up with herbs or harissa or left plain, in all of its garlicky glory. To make a paler, fluffier version of aioli, with a texture that's more pourable, whisk in a tablespoon or two of warm water just before serving.

---

1 egg yolk	1 tablespoon warm water
1 small clove garlic, minced	Fresh lemon juice, to taste
¼ teaspoon kosher salt	Freshly ground black pepper
¾ cup extra-virgin olive oil or a 50-50 mixture of olive and canola oil	

Set a medium mixing bowl on a kitchen towel (this will prevent the bowl from moving as you whisk). Whisk together the egg yolk, garlic, and salt. Whisking constantly, slowly drizzle the oil into the yolk mixture, drop by drop at first, until the mixture begins to thicken, then in a slow, steady stream until all of the oil has been incorporated and the mixture is very thick. Whisk in the warm water to thin the aioli, then season to taste with additional salt, the lemon juice, and black pepper. Serve right away or cover tightly and refrigerate; the aioli will keep for up to 3 days in the refrigerator.

RECIPES USING AIOLI
Grilled Sardines with Aioli (page 61), Small Fish Fry (page 90), Asparagus with Fried Eggs & Aioli (page 121), Chicken-Fried Rabbit (page 215), Horseradish-Walnut Sauce (page 227)

MY THREE BEST BROTHS

It's worth getting into the regular broth making habit. Broth freezes beautifully and adding some to dishes—especially vegetables—enhances their richness and complexity. If you're short on freezer space, you can reduce the broth down and then freeze the super concentrated liquid in ice cube trays. When you need it for a recipe, just dilute it to taste.

ROASTED BIRD BROTH

MAKES ABOUT 3 QUARTS

I like to roast the bones for chicken broth, as the browned bits give the finished broth a nutty complexity absent if you use raw bones. I usually save raw bones in the freezer until I've run out of space, then roast them and make a batch. You can also add the carcasses from roast chickens—go ahead and roast them a second time along with the rest of the bones. I freeze the broth in ice cube trays (for when I just need a small amount) and plastic freezer storage bags, which I lay flat in the freezer so they take up less space.

---

4 pounds raw chicken bones	2 large carrots, peeled and halved crosswise
2 large yellow onions, peeled and quartered	1 tablespoon kosher salt
4 celery stalks, cut into 4-inch pieces	

Preheat the oven to 450°F. Put the bones in a roasting pan and roast for 20 minutes.

Transfer the bones to a large stockpot and add water to cover by 1 inch, then add the onions, celery, carrots, and salt. Bring to a boil, skimming any scum that rises to the surface, then lower the heat so the liquid is gently simmering.

Simmer for 3 to 4 hours, then strain through a fine-mesh sieve into a large bowl and let cool completely; skim off any fat that has risen to the surface. Transfer to jars, cover, and refrigerate. If storing for more than 4 days, transfer the cooled broth to plastic freezer storage bags and lay flat in the freezer. Frozen broth will keep for up to 6 months.

RECIPES USING ROASTED BIRD BROTH
Beef & Pork Ragu (page 128), Squash & Farro Risotto (page 133), Fresh Tomato Risotto (page 134), Easy Seared Mushrooms (page 152), Braised Tripe (page 192), Veal Meatballs (page 206), Chicken Braised in Vinegar and Aromatics (page 207), Beer-Braised Rabbit with Shallots (page 208)

TROTTER BROTH

MAKES ABOUT 3 QUARTS

I first learned of trotter broth from Fergus Henderson's book *The Whole Beast*. It was a revelation for me that something so sweet, mild, and rich could come from something as basic as a pig's foot. You need very little of this broth, which is as firm as Jell-O when cool, to make a big flavor impact. It's the perfect bean cooking liquid, and I'll also add a splash to vegetables, particularly Brussels sprouts, cabbage, and broccoli, which benefit from some porky essence. I also find that adding a small amount of trotter broth to chicken or beef broth improves its texture, making it especially silky and rich.

4 pig's feet	2 carrots, peeled and halved crosswise
2 large yellow onions, peeled and quartered	1 tablespoon kosher salt
4 celery stalks, cut into 4-inch pieces	

Place the pig's feet in a stockpot and add water to cover. Bring to a boil, then drain and rinse the pig's feet in cold water. Rinse out the pot and return the pig's feet to the rinsed pot. Add water to cover by 1 inch, and then add the onions, celery, carrots, and salt. Bring to a boil over high heat, then lower the heat so the liquid is simmering gently.

Simmer for 4 hours, adding water as necessary to keep the pig's feet covered. Strain through a fine-mesh sieve into a large bowl and let cool completely. Transfer the broth to jars, cover, and refrigerate. If you'd like, you can pick the meat from the pig's feet and add it to the broth or keep it separate and combine it with cooked potatoes to make porky hash for breakfast. If storing for more than 4 days, transfer the cooled broth to plastic freezer storage bags and lay flat in the freezer. Frozen broth will keep for up to 6 months.

RECIPES USING TROTTER BROTH
Trotter Beans (page 165), also a great cooking liquid for cabbage and other Brassicas.

CONTINUED

BONE BROTH

MAKES ABOUT 4 QUARTS

This is über broth: simple and nutritious. The long, slow cooking process draws out the nutrients and minerals from the bones, and the rich liquid enhances anything it's added to. You can drink a hot mugful of this as a restorative tonic. For a simple winter lunch, bone broth with a few beaten eggs whisked into it, finished with hot sauce and flaky salt, can't be beat.

---

4 pounds beef bones

2 large yellow onions, peeled and quartered

4 celery stalks, cut into 4-inch pieces

2 carrots, peeled and halved crosswise

1 tablespoon kosher salt

Preheat the oven to 450°F. Put the bones in a roasting pan and roast until well browned, about 30 minutes.

Transfer the bones to a stockpot and add water to cover by 1 inch, then add the onions, celery, carrots, and salt. Bring to a boil, skimming any scum that rises to the surface, then lower the heat so the liquid is gently simmering. Simmer for 4 to 5 hours, adding water as needed to keep the bones mostly covered.

Strain through a fine-mesh sieve into a large bowl and let cool completely; skim off any fat that has risen to the surface. Transfer to jars, cover, and refrigerate. If storing for more than 4 days, transfer the cooled broth to plastic freezer storage bags and lay flat in the freezer. Frozen broth will keep for up to 6 months.

RECIPES USING BONE BROTH
Bright and Fresh Tomato Soup (page 91), Beef & Pork Ragu (page 128), Squash & Farro Risotto (page 133), Fresh Tomato Risotto (page 134)

RENDERED PORK FAT (LARD)

MAKES ABOUT 2 CUPS

Lard was America's most popular fat until it fell out of favor in the 1920s. We cooked our eggs in lard, made piecrusts and pound cakes with it, and fried our chicken in the creamy white fat. Vegetable oil was offered as the substitute, and sadly we took the bait, believing claims that it was more healthful than animal fat. The pendulum has swung back, of course, as it often does, and many now believe that animal fats are more healthful than vegetable oils. Health aside, it has always been more delicious. Use the best pork fat you can find—ideally sourced from a free-ranging animal that has been fed quality feed. The healthier the animal, the better tasting the lard.

1¼ pounds leaf lard or pork fatback	½ cup water

With a sharp knife, trim any blood spots or bits of meat from the lard. Chop the fat into ½-inch cubes. Add the chopped fat and water to a Dutch oven or heavy pot and simmer over medium-low heat, stirring occasionally. After 45 minutes to 1 hour, the water will evaporate, the fat will begin to melt, and the cracklings—little bits of browned fat—will begin to float to the surface of the pot.

Continue to gently stir the melted fat periodically. Eventually the cracklings will sink to the bottom of the pot, at which point you should remove your pot from the heat. Be careful about cooking too far beyond when your cracklings sink—cooking them too much (to the point they are dark brown) will taint your lard with a burnt flavor. Line a fine-mesh sieve with cheesecloth and strain the melted fat into a clean quart-size mason jar, reserving the cracklings for another use (they're especially good on salads).

Let cool completely, then cover the jar and transfer to the refrigerator. The fat will keep, refrigerated, for several months.

RECIPES USING RENDERED PORK FAT (LARD)
Blackened Carrots (page 159), Chicken-Fried Rabbit (page 215), Squab Confit (page 218), Caramelized Apples (page 268), Old-School Pound Cake (with Lard) (page 280)

RENDERED BEEF FAT (TALLOW)

MAKES 1½ CUPS

Tallow, or rendered beef fat, is the hardiest of animal fats. You're not going to want to use this to cook tender greens or spring vegetables—its robust flavor is intense and would be overpowering. But tallow really shines in one application: Tallow Fries (page 169). It was once the chosen frying fat of McDonald's and gives the fries a deeply savory flavor.

1 pound beef fat	⅓ cup water

Preheat the oven to 300°F. Cut the beef fat into ¼-inch cubes, cutting off and discarding any blood, gristle, or meat, and put in a large Dutch oven. Add the water. Put in the oven, uncovered, and stir every 30 to 40 minutes. As the fat melts, impurities will rise to the surface. The tallow is finished when there is clear liquid at the bottom of the pan and the solids on the top begin to brown, about 3 to 4 hours. Pour through a fine-mesh sieve into a clean quart-size mason jar. Let cool completely, then cover and transfer to the refrigerator. The fat will keep, refrigerated, for several months.

RECIPES USING RENDERED BEEF FAT (TALLOW)
Roast Beef with Horseradish-Walnut Sauce (page 226)

CULTURED BUTTER & BUTTERMILK

MAKES ABOUT 1 POUND BUTTER AND 2 CUPS BUTTERMILK

I drink a lot of buttermilk. I remember my mom drinking it by the glassful when I was a kid, so I followed suit, and I'm happy that my daughter also shares this habit. It's often the first thing I consume in the morning, even before coffee—something about the natural cultures in the milk starts me off right.

Buttermilk was once America's national drink, alongside hard cider. It is refreshing and nutritious and provides a dose of good bacteria for your stomach. While kefir has risen in popularity in recent years, I have not seen a parallel growth in buttermilk consumption, probably because it's considered more of a baking ingredient than a beverage. But if you like yogurt and kefir, definitely try drinking buttermilk straight or putting it in a breakfast smoothie; it could become part of your daily routine. Homemade buttermilk tastes slightly zingier than what you'll find in your dairy case.

Homemade butter, particularly cultured butter, has a richer flavor than most of what's commercially available, and if you use best-quality cream, the flavor of the dairy—sweet and tangy—will shine through.

I recognize that making butter and buttermilk is unlikely to become part of anyone's weekly routine, but it can be a fun weekend project or part of the preparation for a pull-out-all-the-stops dinner.

---

6 cups organic heavy cream

¾ cup plain whole milk yogurt

½ teaspoon fine sea salt

In a large bowl, whisk together the cream and yogurt. Cover with a clean kitchen towel and let stand in a warm place for 24 to 36 hours, then transfer to the refrigerator and chill until the mixture reaches 60°F, about 2 hours.

Transfer to the bowl of a stand mixer fitted with the whisk attachment. Start the mixer on a slow speed to avoid spattering, then as the cream starts to thicken, increase the speed to medium. Beat until the mixture separates into thick, pale yellow curds and thin, liquid buttermilk. (Alternatively, you can do this in a food processor. Process on high speed until the curds separate from the liquid, 2 to 3 minutes, then proceed as directed below.)

Line a colander with cheesecloth and set over a bowl. Pour the buttermilk through the cheesecloth, then scrape the curds into the cheesecloth. Gather the ends of the cheesecloth up and around the curds, compressing them into a ball and extracting as much liquid as possible. Pour the buttermilk into a jar and refrigerate; it will keep for up to a week.

Place the butter into the bowl and, using your hands, knead in the salt. Roll into logs, then tightly wrap in plastic wrap and refrigerate; the butter will keep, refrigerated, for a month.

RECIPES USING CULTURED BUTTER & BUTTERMILK
Buttermilk Biscuits (page 65), Bitter Greens with Buttermilk Dressing (page 150), Chicken-Fried Rabbit (page 215), Buttermilk Panna Cotta (page 269), Buttermilk Pie (page 270), or use the cultured butter alongside radishes, or on top of fresh steamed peas.

CANNED TOMATOES

MAKES ABOUT A DOZEN QUARTS

This is a recipe I have developed over many years of tomato canning. In addition to the whole tomatoes, it makes a few jars of a thin, light puree, called *passato* in Italian, which I rely on as a base for ragus and sauces.

This recipe makes a pretty large batch, about 10 quarts of canned tomatoes and some bonus quarts of *passato*. My thought is that if you go to the trouble of getting everything set up, you might as well make a large amount. Juicier tomatoes will yield up to 12 quarts, while drier tomatoes (like dry-farmed ones) could yield as few as eight.

Once you've mastered the basics of canning tomatoes, you can vary the recipe to suit your needs. You can make more jars of *passato* and fewer of whole tomatoes, experiment with canning diced tomatoes, or simmer the *passato* to reduce it before canning, saving you some cooking time later. If you want to make a canned tomato ragu, you can approximate that flavor by reducing the *passato* by half and seasoning to your taste. However, you should never add any fat (like olive oil) to your canned tomatoes, as it may compromise the seal on the jar.

If you want to use quart jars, buy a dozen; if you prefer pints, buy two dozen. Sterilize the jars before using, either by briefly dunking the jars in boiling water or running them through the dishwasher on hot without soap. You'll also need a pressure canner or a large pot 3 inches taller than your jars and a trivet or circular cooling rack. This project will take at least 3 hours start to finish, and it's way more fun to do with two or three people, as doing it by yourself can be tiresome.

---

1 case (20 to 24 pounds) sauce tomatoes (Roma or San Marzano), ripe but not soft

1 tablespoon kosher salt

Juice of 1 lemon

Bring a large pot of water to a boil over high heat. Rinse the tomatoes in cold water and separate them into two even piles. Any tomatoes that have green spots, soft spots, or blemishes should go in the "Grade B" pile; put the best-looking tomatoes in the "Grade A" pile (if all of your tomatoes are perfect—lucky you—just divide into two even piles anyway, as half will be kept whole and half pureed).

Working in batches, transfer some of the Grade B tomatoes to the boiling water and boil for 2 to 3 minutes per batch, until they are soft enough that the flesh gives easily when squeezed. With a spider or slotted spoon, transfer the blanched tomatoes to a bowl and repeat with the remaining Grade B tomatoes, allowing the water to return to a boil between each batch.

With the tip of a sharp knife, score an *X* in the bottom of each Grade A tomato. In a large pot or your empty, clean sink, prepare an ice bath.

Working in batches, transfer the Grade A tomatoes to the boiling water and blanch for about 90 seconds—the skin should start peeling back just a little around the score lines. You do not want to overcook them, or they will be mushy. If the tomatoes are very firm, they can take up to 2 minutes, while a riper batch can take less than a minute. With a spider or slotted spoon, remove the tomatoes from the boiling water and transfer to the ice water bath. Repeat with the remaining Grade A tomatoes, letting the water return to a boil between batches and adding more water to the pot as necessary.

Put a food mill over a large bowl. Run the blanched Grade B tomatoes through a tomato mill or a food mill's finest setting—you can use the coarser setting, but the puree will have more seeds. If you want to speed up the process somewhat, you can first pulse the tomatoes briefly in a food processor; it makes the milling work easier, but results in another dirty appliance.

When all of the Grade B tomatoes have been milled, add the salt and lemon juice to the puree.

Peel the Grade A tomatoes and place in a bowl, it should slip off easily. If it doesn't, you can drop them back in your boiling water bath for a minute or two until they are easy to peel (but not so long they become mushy).

Fill the sterile mason jars with the whole, peeled Grade A tomatoes, packing the tomatoes into the jars tightly but leaving about 1 inch of space at the top of each jar; you will not have enough whole tomatoes to fill all the jars; the remaining jars will be filled with surplus tomato puree. With a clean paper towel, wipe the rim of each jar to ensure absolutely nothing will touch the rubber part of the flat canning lid, which can prevent the jar from sealing properly and lead to spoilage.

Using a canning funnel, ladle the tomato puree into the jars containing the whole tomatoes, leaving about ¾ inch of space at the top of each jar. Once you have filled all the jars with whole tomatoes, pour any surplus puree into the remaining (empty) jars. Wipe the rims of each jar again with a clean paper towel.

Put the lids on the jars and screw a band onto each to close. Don't worry about making the bands supertight, as the band is not what seals the jar; it's the vacuum seal formed by the lid that does. If you really tighten those bands, all you do is make the jars harder to open later on.

Transfer the jars to a pressure canner and follow the manufacturer's instructions for processing tomatoes. If you do not have a pressure canner, the canned tomatoes can also be processed in a boiling water bath. Take your largest pot—which must be at least 3 inches taller than your tallest jar—and fill halfway with water. Put a trivet or a round wire cooling rack in the bottom of the pot. Bring the water to a boil and carefully lower your canned tomatoes into the boiling water (canning tongs can be useful for transferring the jars). If the water does not cover the jars by at least 1 inch, add water until it does. Once the water returns to a rolling boil, start timing: pints should boil for 25 minutes, quarts for 45 minutes. Add more water as necessary so the jars are covered with water for the entire cooking time.

Remove your jars from the pressure canner or the boiling water bath and let cool. They will keep for up to 2 years in a cool, dark place, but I always find I'm finishing up the last of the prior year's canned tomatoes just as fresh ones come back into season.

RECIPES USING CANNED TOMATOES
Bright and Fresh Tomato Soup (page 91), Beef & Pork Ragu (page 128), Stuffed Zucchini Blossoms in Tomato Sauce (page 138), Squid & Beans (page 190), Agrodolce Tongue (page 191), Braised Tripe (page 192), Beef Involtini with Ham & Provolone (page 224)

THREE GREEN SAUCES

MAKES ABOUT 1½ CUPS

I am pretty sure that green sauce migrated from Italy to South America, but its existence on both continents might be another example of convergent evolution on our culinary planet. The sauce's function is the same across both cultures: it acts as a foil for rich protein, cutting through the fat and adding a bright herbaceous element to a dish.

Back when I was living in Italy, lunch would often be a plate spread with a thin layer of green sauce, topped with two halved hard-boiled eggs and a few anchovy fillets, served with a side of bread. When I worked in Uruguay, every night's meal featured a grilled piece of meat with a ladleful of chimichurri on the side. These are great condiments, although I am never a fan of marinating meats in any type of green sauce, as heat ruins the fresh herb flavors.

I pair these sauces with everything from grilled steaks, roasted pork loin, and roasted chicken to boiled cauliflower or fried eggs. To make this into a main dish, spread a quarter-inch layer on a plate and top with sliced boiled eggs, anchovies, and pitted olives and scoop up with a baguette or crackers.

SALSA VERDE

This is a mild and well-balanced green sauce that is great as a starter, topped with boiled eggs and anchovy fillets, or served alongside mild meats like boiled or grilled chicken. The more traditional Italian chefs insist on using only the leaves of the herbs—no stalks—and cutting them all by hand with a mezzaluna. But the new-fashioned way of whizzing the herbs in the food processor, stems and all, makes an equally delicious sauce.

2 eggs	¾ cup extra-virgin olive oil
1 bunch Italian parsley, large stems removed	½ cup capers
1 small bunch fresh basil, large stems removed	2 teaspoons red wine vinegar
	1 teaspoon red pepper flakes
4 anchovy fillets (optional)	½ teaspoon kosher salt

Place the eggs in a small saucepan and cover with cold water. Bring to a boil, cover, remove from the heat, and let stand for 9 minutes. Transfer to an ice water bath and, when cool enough to handle, peel. Cut the eggs in half and remove the yolks (the whites can be discarded or eaten as a cook's snack).

In a food processor, combine the egg yolks, parsley, basil, anchovy fillets, olive oil, capers, vinegar, red pepper flakes, and salt. Process until smooth. Let stand at room temperature for at least 1 hour before serving. The sauce will keep, refrigerated, for up to 2 days; let come to room temperature before serving.

CONTINUED

TRADITIONAL URUGUAYAN CHIMICHURRI

This recipe is a modification of one I learned from the great Uruguayan chef Santiago Garat. I love this chimi on grilled leaner meats, like a flatiron steak or *picanha*, a cut from the rump of a cow that's popular in Brazil and Uruguay.

1½ cups packed fresh parsley leaves

4 cloves garlic, coarsely chopped

2 tablespoons packed fresh oregano leaves

1½ tablespoons packed fresh rosemary leaves

1 tablespoon packed fresh thyme leaves

1 fresh bay leaf

1 teaspoon red pepper flakes

¾ cup extra-virgin olive oil

⅓ cup sherry vinegar

Kosher salt

Freshly ground black pepper

In a food processor, combine the parsley, garlic, oregano, rosemary, thyme, bay leaf, and red pepper flakes. Pulse until the herbs are finely chopped. Add the olive oil and vinegar and pulse to combine. Season the chimichurri to taste with salt and pepper and transfer to a bowl. Let stand for at least 1 hour before serving. The sauce will keep, refrigerated, for up to 2 days; let come to room temperature before serving.

ROUGH CHIMICHURRI

This version is essentially halfway between the Italian and Uruguayan versions, the minor innovation being that I leave most of the leaves whole. I love the look and texture of the resulting rough chimi.

½ cup fine dry bread crumbs

¼ cup red wine vinegar

¼ cup water

4 anchovy fillets

4 cloves garlic, smashed

1 bunch Italian parsley, stemmed

1 loosely packed cup fresh oregano leaves

1 cup extra-virgin olive oil

Kosher salt

In a medium bowl, combine the bread crumbs, vinegar, and water and let stand for 10 minutes. Put the anchovy fillets and garlic in a pile on a large cutting board and, with a sharp knife, finely chop into a paste. Place the parsley and oregano leaves on top of the anchovy-garlic paste and chop just to combine; you want the herbs to remain largely intact.

Transfer the herb-garlic mixture to the bowl containing the soaked bread crumbs and stir to combine. Pour in the olive oil and season to taste with salt. Let stand for at least 1 hour before serving. The sauce will keep, refrigerated, for up to 2 days; let come to room temperature before serving.

RECIPES USING GREEN SAUCES

Chicken-Fried Rabbit (page 215), Roast Beef with Horseradish-Walnut Sauce (page 226), Rack of Goat or Lamb (page 228), Simple Seared Beef Heart (page 230), also try it alongside boiled eggs, spread on sandwiches, or on top of any grilled meat.

BAGNA CAUDA

MAKES ABOUT 1 CUP

Bagna cauda is one of my favorite condiments, as I believe that the combination of fat, garlic, and anchovies is the three-legged stool on which so many great dishes are built. I also believe (though maybe somewhat erroneously) that it's something of a health tonic, given the combined powers of garlic and omega-3-rich fish and olive oil, all further improved by the addition of butter.

The name *bagna cauda*, or "hot bath," refers to both a sauce and a specific way of serving the sauce with a selection of crudités. Serving bagna cauda alongside raw vegetables is derived from the traditional midday meal of Piedmont, Italy. Parallel to the old American country tradition of a hearty midday supper followed by a light dinner, the Piedmontese farmers of yore would head out to work early in the morning and come home around noon to meals of raw vegetables, bread, or chunks of leftover polenta dipped into warm cups of anchovies, garlic, and butter.

This traditional preparation is great and a fun thing to serve at a wintry dinner party, when vegetables like radicchio, fennel, radishes, and cauliflower, all particularly complemented by the sauce, are in season. To do this, you'll need a fondue pot with a heat source beneath to keep the sauce warm, or you can purchase a terra-cotta bagna cauda pot made exclusively for this purpose. The vessel is important: without it, the sauce will cool and congeal unappealingly.

For a more everyday way to enjoy this sauce, I use it as a salad dressing for sturdy greens like kale, escarole, and radicchio (see Seared Radicchio with Bagna Cauda, page 160); toss it with warm roasted root vegetables; spoon it over grilled meats like squab or goat; or use it to dress up leftover roasted meat like roast beef.

10 salt-cured anchovies	½ cup extra-virgin olive oil
3 small heads garlic	½ cup (1 stick) unsalted butter, cubed
1 cup milk	Kosher salt

Put the anchovies in a bowl, cover with cold water, and let soak for 30 minutes. Drain and pull the anchovies into halves, discarding the bones and setting the fillets aside.

Separate the heads of garlic into cloves but do not peel them. Place the whole, unpeeled garlic cloves into a small saucepan and add the milk. Bring to a boil over medium-high heat, then lower to a simmer and simmer until the cloves are tender, about 15 minutes. Drain, discarding the milk.

Pass the garlic and anchovy fillets through the widest setting of a food mill. If you do not have a food mill, peel the garlic before boiling in milk. Once the garlic is cooked, mash the garlic and anchovies together in a mortar and pestle into a chunky paste.

Transfer the garlic-anchovy paste to a medium pot set on a diffuser over very low heat, and add the olive oil and butter. If you do not have a diffuser but have an electric stove, just use the lowest setting on your electric stove. If you have a gas range but no diffuser, set a cast-iron frying pan directly on the burner then put the saucepan on top. Cook for at least 30 minutes or up to 2 hours. The mixture should never bubble or brown; if it does, lower the heat.

Season with salt. The bagna cauda is now ready to use. If serving as a dip for vegetables, pour the sauce into a fondue or bagna cauda pot and set over a candle to keep warm. Bagna cauda can be made a day ahead and gently reheated before using. Leftover bagna cauda will keep, refrigerated, for a week.

RECIPES USING BAGNA CAUDA
Seared Radicchio with Bagna Cauda (page 160), Roast Beef with Horseradish-Walnut Sauce (page 226), also great paired with any raw or boiled vegetable, as a dressing for robust cooked greens, or drizzled over toasts topped with fresh cheese.

BARBADIAN HOT SAUCE

MAKES ABOUT 3 CUPS

For the past few years I have been planning and building a farm-to-bottle rum business in Punta Gorda, Belize, where my company, Belcampo, has a farm and eco-lodge. The farm we now manage has a history of rum production, but it hasn't grown cane or produced liquor for nearly a century. To get a sense of all the work ahead, my business partner and I made a few trips to famous rum distilleries in the French West Indies that make *agricole* rum from fresh, whole sugarcane juice, rather than using molasses or other sugar by-products, as some companies do. (It's a tough job, but someone has to do it.)

These adventures took me to Barbados for the first time, where I was inspired by the jars of vinegary hot sauce on every table. Served alongside platefuls of little fried fish fritters and rich Barbadian dishes, this hot sauce has a dual effect of adding spice but magically making everything a bit more digestible. Turmeric, a root that is said to have all sorts of amazing medicinal properties, gives the sauce an earthy flavor.

You can use the sauce right after it's made, but it improves with age; I like to let it mellow for a few weeks after I make it, so the flavors meld and the sauce becomes less piquant and spicy.

¼ pound fresh turmeric root, peeled and diced

1 to 1½ cups white vinegar

1 small white onion, coarsely chopped

½ pound Scotch bonnet or habanero chiles, stems removed

¼ cup Dijon mustard

1 tablespoon brown sugar

Kosher salt

Put the turmeric in the bowl of the food processer or blender and process until almost smooth, adding some of the vinegar if necessary to aid the blending. Add the onion and process until finely chopped, then add the chiles and continue processing until the mixture has a bit of texture but no large pieces of onion or chile.

Transfer to a medium nonreactive bowl and add 1 cup of the vinegar, the mustard, and sugar. Taste the sauce. If it's too spicy for your liking, add a bit more vinegar, mustard, and sugar and taste again, but note that as it ages its flavor will mellow. The sauce should have a pourable consistency; add more vinegar if it's too thick. Using a funnel, transfer the sauce into sterilized jars or bottles and cap tightly. Though you can eat it right away, the sauce gets better with age and will last up to a year stored in a cool, dark place. Season to taste with salt.

RECIPES USING BARBADIAN HOT SAUCE
Use it as a topping on the Olive Oil Crackers (page 66), with Oil-Packed Sardines (page 61), or add it to scrambled eggs or as a condiment on a cheese plate.

WELCOME

SNACKS, STARTERS & COCKTAILS

I like to feed my guests well, beginning the moment they arrive. That said, it's my belief that snacks and starters should be casual bites, not labor-intensive and not so substantial that they overshadow the meal, but flavor packed and well considered, something delicious that's a preview of the rest of the dinner. We can always revert to a big bowl of olives or nuts, but I think that making a snack that feels a bit special, and shows that you took some care, sets a nice tone for dinner and also takes some pressure off of the main course.

Over the years I've mastered a short list of things I can make on the fly, easy and simple ways to kick off a meal or fun little dishes to serve alongside drinks: blistered, flaky cheese-filled *focaccia di recco*, tiny fried fish with aioli, roasted red pepper and anchovy "rollmops," and crispy homemade crackers. If I'm serving cocktails, I almost always mix up a large batch in a mason jar and just shake and pour over ice.

For a mix of starters, I usually have something bready, something vegetable based, and something with meat or eggs. For the bready and meat/egg options, you'll find all of my favorites in the following pages. For the vegetables, I usually just follow what's in season: quartered ripe tomatoes with salt, whole small fava bean pods blistered on the grill, or a bowl of radishes with butter and salt. I usually try to avoid plates and utensils for starters and just leave a jar of forks and a stack of napkins near the food, saving one round of cleanup and making it easier to transition to dinner.

SNACKS, STARTERS & COCKTAILS

CARNE CRUDA

SERVES 6 TO 8

Carne cruda takes me to a really happy place. I used to think I was the only person on earth who liked raw beef: I snuck big pinches of ground meat from the package when I was a little kid. I would sprinkle a glob of raw beef with salt and gobble it down. I always thought I took so little and was so sneaky that my mom would never notice. I realize now that was probably not the case.

When I moved to Italy in my twenties, I discovered the Piemontese tradition of eating raw beef. There, *carne cruda* is a daily staple, as popular as burgers are Stateside. I typically make Italian-style raw beef, using unaged eye of round and seasoning it with only salt, olive oil, and lemon juice. But I'll admit a fondness for the French-style tartare, too—if you share that fondness, feel free to garnish the meat with the optional condiments: minced red onion, capers, and hard-boiled egg yolks.

This was my daughter's first food—clearly she comes by her love of raw meat honestly. As long as you are sure of the quality of the beef, it's a great high-protein snack for kids.

---

2 pounds beef eye of round (other cuts I use regularly are top round and London broil)

½ cup water

½ cup extra-virgin olive oil, plus more for drizzling

½ cup lemon juice

1 tablespoon kosher salt

1 clove garlic

Minced red onion (optional)

Minced capers (optional)

Crumbled hard-boiled egg yolk (optional)

Crackers or toasts, for serving (optional)

With a sharp knife, trim the beef of all fat, sinew, and silver skin. Transfer the meat to a plate, then put in the freezer for 15 minutes (this will make the meat easier to chop).

Finely chop the beef, transfer to a medium bowl, and refrigerate until very cold. Alternatively, you

can cube the chilled meat, then pass it through the coarse die of a meat grinder.

Remove the meat from the refrigerator and stir in the water, olive oil, lemon juice, and salt.

Slice the garlic clove in half and rub the cut side of the clove over the surface of a serving platter. Pile the *carne cruda* onto the platter and drizzle with a ribbon of olive oil. Serve cold, accompanied by onion, caper, and egg yolk garnishes or with crackers (page 66) or toasts.

SEARED LAMB HEART CRUDO

SERVES 4

This dish was inspired by an epic dinner at the Belcampo farm, when our culinary team competed to develop recipes using our most challenging cuts of meat—all delicious but in need of a marketing campaign. Lamb hearts, while popular elsewhere in the world, are not my company's best sellers, no doubt in part because no one knows how to cook them. This recipe—in which the hearts are seared but left raw within, then chopped and served as you would beef tartare—won me over.

2 lamb hearts

1 teaspoon kosher salt

1 tablespoon extra-virgin olive oil

1 teaspoon lemon juice

Freshly ground black pepper

1 whole lemon, quartered, for serving

Flaky salt, such as Maldon, for serving

Trim all the fat and visible membranes from the exteriors of the hearts, then butterfly each heart, taking care not to cut all the way through, and open them flat like a book; discard any visible fat and membranes from the interior. Season each heart with half of the salt and let stand at room temperature for 10 minutes.

Heat a small cast-iron pan over high heat until it is blazing hot. Add the hearts and sear for 1 minute on each side. Transfer to a cutting board and chop very finely. Transfer to a bowl and add the olive oil and lemon juice and stir to combine. Season to taste with additional salt and pepper and serve with the quartered lemon and flaky salt on the side.

CHICKEN HEARTS COOKED IN BROWN BUTTER

SERVES 6

Like so many offal dishes, chicken hearts should never be cooked beyond medium-rare, after which point they become chewy and unpleasant. You should aspire to a heart that's sizzling brown on the outside and pink within.

I keep a couple of half-pint containers of chicken hearts in the freezer—they thaw quickly under warm running water, making this a great last-minute meaty starter for a vegetable-heavy meal. I usually plan for about three hearts per person, which guarantees you won't have leftovers. If my daughter is in attendance, I need to make at least five for her—it's probably her favorite meat dish after lamb chops.

---

2 tablespoon unsalted butter

1½ cups chicken hearts

Flaky salt, such as Maldon, for serving

In a small cast-iron skillet over medium-high heat, melt the butter. When the milk solids are beginning to brown and the butter has a rich, nutty smell, add the chicken hearts and cook, tossing them around in the pan as if you're making popcorn, until browned on all sides, no more than 2 minutes. Remove from the pan with a slotted spoon, sprinkle with flaky salt, and serve immediately.

FRESH RICOTTA

MAKES 3 CUPS/1½ POUNDS

My friend Angelo Garro—cook, hunter, metalsmith—
taught me this technique of making ricotta at home.
This version uses whole milk and produces a dense and
creamy cheese. Fresh ricotta is one of my workhorse
ingredients, something I always like to have around. I use
it in recipes, like the Panzerotti (page 74) and Savory-
Sweet Ricotta Cheesecake (page 279), and often serve
ricotta as a stand-alone appetizer: take a slice of well-
drained ricotta and sear it in olive oil until dark golden
on each side, sprinkle it with salt, and serve on bread or
with just a fork, drizzled with more olive oil. Or serve a
bowl of ricotta drizzled with olive oil and topped with
cracked black pepper, accompanied by crudités and
garlic-rubbed toasts.

1 gallon whole milk (not ultra-pasteurized)	⅓ cup white vinegar
	¼ teaspoon fine sea salt

Pour the milk into a large nonreactive saucepan over
medium heat and stir occasionally until it reaches
180°F. Remove from the heat and stir in the vinegar
and salt. Let stand at room temperature for 1 hour, at
which point the curds and whey will have separated.

Line a colander with a few layers of cheesecloth
and place it over a large bowl. Pour the curds and
whey into the colander and let the curds strain for
at least 1 hour. After 1 hour, you'll have a tender
but spreadable ricotta. After 2 hours, it will be
spreadable but firmer, almost like cream cheese.
(It will firm as it cools, so do not judge its final
texture by what you have in your cheesecloth.) Eat
the ricotta right away or transfer it to an airtight
container and refrigerate until ready to use. Ricotta
will keep, refrigerated, for 3 days.

TOMA CHEESE WITH GREEN HERBS

MAKES 1 POUND

My first food job was manual labor in a dairy in Wales, making Caerphilly cheese (a hard cow's milk cheese). I enjoyed rising with the sun and breathing in the sweet smell of warm milk all day long. And while I loved the final aged cheese we produced, I also adored eating the fresh curd for lunch on bread. This fresh, simple cheese tastes of fresh sweet milk, as that is pretty much all it is—a soft block of lightly salted curd brightened with herbs. You'll need rennet to coagulate the proteins in the milk. You can purchase animal rennet, which is made from an enzyme found in the stomachs of cows, goats, and sheep; vegetarian rennet, derived from plants, is also available. Both are inexpensive and can be ordered online. Make sure to read the ratio on the rennet you buy—the strength of different brands varies widely.

The cheese will keep for a few days, refrigerated, or you can extend its life up to a month or so by packing small cubes of it into a jar and adding olive oil to cover. Serve it with toasts or crackers.

---

1 gallon whole milk
(not ultra-pasteurized)

½ teaspoon rennet

½ cup fresh herbs, such as basil, parsley, and chervil, or a combination, finely chopped

2 tablespoons kosher salt

In a heavy pot over medium heat, heat the milk until warm to the touch, around 100° to 125°F. Remove from the heat, add the rennet, and let stand for 45 minutes, until curds have formed. Do not stir.

Line a colander with cheesecloth and set the colander over a bowl near your work area. Return the pot of milk to low heat and, with a long knife, cut the curds into a tic-tac-toe shape. Cook, gently stirring occasionally, until the curds begin to clump together and the whey has distinctly separated, about 12 minutes. Stir in the herbs, then pour into the colander.

Gather the cheesecloth around the curds, squeezing hard to expel the whey, then sprinkle with salt. Form the cheese into a disk, using the cheesecloth as a wrapper, and put on a rimmed baking sheet. Top with a second baking sheet and weight it down with a brick, book, or other heavy, flat object. Transfer to the refrigerator and let stand for at least 1 hour or up to overnight.

Cut into small pieces and serve or transfer the cubes to a mason jar and add extra-virgin olive oil to cover. The cheese will keep, tightly wrapped and refrigerated, for up to 3 days. If you have packed the cheese in oil, let it come to room temperature before serving.

FORMAGETTO

MAKES ABOUT 1 POUND

This is an easy cheese to make at home but yields an impressive result: a soft, creamy cheese that can be used in myriad ways, including as a topping for bruschetta or salads. Because this cheese is made with a small amount of rennet to coagulate the milk, it forms more delicate curds that have a lightly acidic flavor, bolstered by the natural bacteria culture (and flavor) of yogurt. This is a type of cheese I learned to make when I was a cheese maker in Italy, and it's a very popular product in the local markets in central and northern Italy—smeared on morning toast or as an ingredient in *crostata*, savory tarts, or as a filling for fresh pasta.

1 gallon whole milk	Rennet (amount varies by brand; expect to use ⅛ to ¼ teaspoon)
1 cup whole milk yogurt	
	2 teaspoons kosher salt

In a large heavy pot over medium heat, warm the milk until it's body temperature—about 98°F. When the milk is warm, remove from the heat and whisk in the yogurt. Each brand of rennet is a bit different, but all come with instructions that tell you how much should be added to coagulate a certain volume of milk. For this cheese, you should add *half* the amount of rennet advised for a gallon of milk (because rennet varies I cannot give an exact amount, but it's typically between ¼ and ½ teaspoon per gallon of milk) and whisk to combine. Let stand at room temperature for at least 4 hours or overnight.

Line a colander with wet cheesecloth and set over a bowl. With a slotted spoon, gently spoon the curds into the colander, taking care not to agitate the curd or stir it, which will make the cheese gummy. Every third scoop, sprinkle the curds with some of the salt, distributing evenly. Let drain in the refrigerator for 4 hours, then transfer to a bowl. The cheese will keep in the refrigerator, tightly wrapped, for 1 week.

ANCHOVIES TWO WAYS

SERVES 4 TO 6

One of my favorite ways to prepare fresh anchovies
is to cure the fish with acid—either vinegar or lemon
juice—then serve the cured fillets on pieces of toast
as a simple snack or add them to salads. If scaling,
gutting, and beheading the tiny fish is too much
of a hassle, try the Small Fish Fry (page 90),
which uses whole anchovies instead. I typically
clean as many fish as I have patience for and
then fry the remainder.

SIMPLE MARINATED ANCHOVIES

20 small fresh anchovies (about 1 pound)

1 teaspoon kosher salt

White wine vinegar

2 cloves garlic, sliced paper-thin

2 tablespoons fresh parsley, finely chopped

Extra-virgin olive oil

Using scissors, trim the fins off of all of the anchovies. Gut the fish using a sharp paring knife, and rinse well. Cut off the heads and carefully remove the spine bones by pulling starting from the tail. Separate the 2 fillets and rinse again.

Spread the fillets on a deep plate or large shallow bowl in a single layer and sprinkle with the salt. Add enough vinegar to cover, then let marinate, refrigerated, for 4 hours.

Rinse the anchovies in cold water and drain on paper towels, drying the fish carefully. Arrange a single layer of anchovies on a plate and sprinkle with garlic and parsley. Continue layering anchovies, garlic, and parsley, ending with a layer of fish. Add a generous pour of olive oil over the top, enough to cover the fish. Cover tightly with plastic wrap and refrigerate for at least 1 hour. Bring to room temperature before serving. The anchovies will keep, refrigerated, for up to 2 weeks, provided they are covered with a layer of olive oil.

LEMON-CURED ANCHOVIES

20 small fresh anchovies (about 1 pound)

½ cup fresh lemon juice

1 teaspoon kosher salt

1 teaspoon red pepper flakes

Toasts, for serving

Extra-virgin olive oil, for serving

Prepare the anchovies as in the first step of Simple Marinated Anchovies. In a small bowl, whisk together the lemon juice, salt, and red pepper flakes. Add the fillets to a glass pint jar in any orientation or lay on a plate in a single layer.

Pour the lemon juice mixture over and let stand for at least 4 hours, which will yield a ceviche-like half-cooked texture, or for up to 1 week, refrigerated, which will fully "cook" the fish. Serve the fish on toasts, drizzled with extra-virgin olive oil.

SARDINES
TWO WAYS

SERVES 4

Sardines are one of my favorite fish. Not only are they plentiful and inexpensive, but I also like how their dense, rich flesh is complemented by so many delicious sauces: green sauces (page 27), romesco, or just a bright gremolata made with citrus zest and parsley.

Sardines are most often found canned rather than fresh, in part because all of the oil in the flesh causes the meat to become soft and mealy after just a few days out of the water. But recently, fresh sardines have become more widely available as their health benefits are celebrated and as concern about mercury and the viability of predator species has caused chefs and home cooks to look to smaller, more sustainable fish. Buy them from a fishmonger you trust and who can assure you of the sardines' age. The two on the facing page are my favorite ways to prepare the fish. The first, packed in oil, tastes best when the fish are on the smaller side. The second, whole grilled sardines, works with fish of any size.

OIL-PACKED SARDINES

8 small sardines, heads on, scaled and gutted

Kosher salt

2 cups extra-virgin olive oil

2 lemon wheels

Handful of parsley sprigs

1 teaspoon red pepper flakes

Rinse the sardines in cold water and dry thoroughly inside and out with paper towels. Sprinkle a healthy pinch of salt in the cavity of each fish. Place the sardines in a cast-iron pan large enough to hold them all in a single layer and pour the olive oil over. Place the pan over medium heat and cook until the oil begins to bubble slightly. Let cook for 1 minute more, then turn off the heat and add the lemon wheels, parsley, and red pepper flakes.

Let stand until the oil comes to room temperature, then transfer the sardines to a jar or terrine and pour the oil over; the sardines should be completely covered with oil. Remove the parsley. Refrigerate overnight or for up to 1 week. Bring to room temperature before serving.

GRILLED SARDINES WITH AIOLI

8 sardines, heads on, scaled and gutted

2 tablespoons canola oil

2 tablespoons fresh parsley leaves

Flaky sea salt, such as Maldon, for serving

Aioli (page 17), for serving

Rinse the sardines in cold water and dry thoroughly inside and out with paper towels. Place a large cast-iron pan over high heat and heat until wisps of smoke rise from the pan. Add the oil, and when the oil is hot, lay the sardines in the pan in a single layer (depending on the size of your pan, you may need to do this in batches). Fry on one side until the skin is dark brown, about 2 minutes, then flip and fry on the other side for 1 to 2 minutes more.

Transfer to a serving platter and scatter the parsley leaves over and sprinkle with flaky salt. Serve warm, accompanied by aioli.

PICKLED GRAPES

MAKES 3 PINTS

I am a sucker for a simple pickle, and these grapes—
which can be assembled in less than 10 minutes, start
to finish, and are ready to eat the next day—are a fine
example. They walk the line between sweet and savory
and are an excellent accompaniment to charcuterie and
cheese. Since commercial grapes are heavily sprayed,
seek out organically grown fruit. You'll need three pint-
size canning jars with lids.

---

2 pounds organic seedless
grapes (about 6 cups), green,
red, black, or a mixture,
stemmed

3 sprigs fresh tarragon

3 cloves garlic, crushed

2 cups white wine vinegar

1 cup water

½ cup sugar

2 tablespoons kosher salt

Pack the grapes into the pint jars. Add a sprig of
tarragon and a garlic clove to each jar. In a small
saucepan over medium heat, combine the vinegar,
water, sugar, and salt. Bring to a simmer, stirring to
dissolve the sugar and salt, then pour the hot brine
over the grapes.

Let cool to room temperature, then cover tightly
and refrigerate. The grapes are ready to eat in
1 day but will keep, refrigerated, for 1 month.
Serve alongside confits, pâté, or other rich meats.

LIVER PÂTÉ

MAKES ABOUT 2 CUPS

This recipe can be made from the livers of chickens, ducks, geese—or a mixture of all three. The important thing here is to use very fresh livers that have never been frozen, as I find that frozen livers often develop a harsh, metallic flavor that can ruin a delicate pâté. The recipe can be scaled down or up, so you can adjust the recipe based on how much fresh liver you are able to get from your butcher. If you'd like, you can cut the heavy cream from this recipe. The result will be a little less elegant, a little more rustic, but still very delicious.

8 tablespoons (1 stick) unsalted butter, cut into cubes

2 shallots, finely chopped

2 cups fresh chicken, duck, or goose livers (a mixture also is fine) (approximately 1 pound)

1 tablespoon fresh thyme leaves

⅓ cup Madeira or port

3 tablespoons heavy cream, plus more as needed

Kosher salt

In a large, heavy sauté pan over medium heat, melt 4 tablespoons of the butter. Add the shallots and sauté until translucent, stirring, about 4 minutes. Do not let the shallots brown.

Add the livers, thyme, and Madeira and increase the heat to medium-high. Cook, stirring occasionally, until the wine has reduced and the livers are lightly browned but still very soft and pink on the inside, 3 to 5 minutes.

Transfer the liver mixture to a food processor and add the cream and remaining 4 tablespoons butter. Puree until smooth, adding more cream as necessary. Season with salt. Transfer to a bowl and smooth the top with a spatula. Serve warm or at room temperature. The pâté will keep, tightly wrapped, for up to 5 days. If storing for more than a few hours, press a sheet of plastic wrap directly onto the surface of the pâté (this will prevent discoloration); bring to room temperature before serving.

BUTTERMILK BISCUITS

MAKES 6 LARGE BISCUITS

I learned everything I know about buttermilk biscuits while working for a summer as a baker on a dude ranch in Montana, on the outskirts of Yellowstone. I baked for a crew of a few dozen locals as well as the sixty or so guests that were at the hotel every day. Buttermilk biscuits with sausage gravy were often on the menu, and I still remember coming across a hungover cowboy one morning, standing in the walk-in refrigerator, trying to drink cold gravy from a gravy boat. He was shaking the boat over his open mouth, waiting for a chunk to fall in.

Making buttermilk biscuits twice a day, every day, for a few months is great training. You start to understand the feel of good biscuit dough; as with pie dough, repetition is the best teacher. What I learned after making this dough a few hundred times is that it should be wet enough to hold together but not so wet that it's tacky and goopy; a shaggy dough ball ensures flaky, tender biscuits. These can be stamped out with a biscuit cutter or formed into drop biscuits, and both are best eaten the same day they're baked, preferably while still warm.

2¼ cups all-purpose flour	½ teaspoon kosher salt
1½ tablespoons baking powder	8 tablespoons (1 stick) cold unsalted butter, cut into small pieces
¾ teaspoon baking soda	1 cup buttermilk (page 23)

Preheat the oven to 400°F. In a medium bowl, whisk together the flour, baking powder, baking soda, and salt. With a pastry cutter or your fingers, work the butter into the flour mixture until the mixture resembles coarse cornmeal (a few larger pieces of butter are okay).

Stir in the buttermilk with a fork and knead very gently in the bowl until the dough comes together into a shaggy ball. Transfer to a work surface and pat into a ½-inch-thick disk. With a 2½-inch biscuit cutter, cut the dough into six rounds. Gather the scraps together and press them into a disk a second time in order to cut all six biscuits; be as gentle as possible.

Transfer the biscuits to an unlined baking sheet and bake until puffed and golden, 12 to 14 minutes. To make drop biscuits, add an extra ½ cup of buttermilk to the dough and use a large spoon to scoop and drop dough onto an unlined baking sheet, spacing mounds about 2 inches apart; bake as directed above. Transfer to a wire rack and let cool slightly—the biscuits are best eaten warm.

Note: If you'd like to make smaller biscuits, use a 1½-inch cutter to stamp out a dozen biscuits. Bake for 8 to 10 minutes.

OLIVE OIL CRACKERS

MAKES ABOUT 60 CRACKERS

In my opinion, most spreads and dips taste best on a crispy cracker. Problem is, most crackers are made from hyperprocessed ingredients that you don't want to eat, and boxes of so-called artisanal crackers will run you $12 for a handful. So I started making my own—twice as delicious as store-bought at a fraction of the cost. The key to crisp crackers is rolling the dough extremely thin, which, admittedly, can be a pain. My trick is to multitask: I roll the dough into a circle, then do something else for about 5 minutes, roll the circle to double the circumference, then do something else—every time you pause, the dough relaxes and your work gets much easier.

These crackers keep for a week packed in a paper bag. Don't store them in a plastic bag, or they will soften. If your crackers lose their crispness, you can pop them back into a hot oven for a few minutes to recrisp.

---

1 cup whole wheat flour

1 cup all-purpose flour

½ cup warm water

1 tablespoon olive oil, plus more for brushing on crackers

1 teaspoon kosher salt, plus more for sprinkling on crackers

In a stand mixer fitted with a dough hook, combine the flours, water, olive oil, and salt. Mix on medium speed until smooth and elastic, about 15 minutes (this can also be done by hand). The dough should be very stiff and not at all sticky; if necessary, add a bit more flour by the tablespoonful until it is no longer sticky.

Cover the bowl with plastic wrap or a clean kitchen towel and let stand at room temperature for 1 hour (at this point the dough can also be tightly wrapped with plastic wrap and refrigerated for up to 3 days).

Preheat the oven to 350°F. Transfer the dough to a floured work surface and cut into four pieces. With a floured rolling pin, working with one piece of dough at a time, roll the dough as thinly as possible. Using a sharp knife or pizza cutter, cut into 3 by 1-inch rectangles. Transfer to two parchment-lined baking sheets (the crackers do not spread, so you do not need to leave much space between them) and brush each cracker on both sides with olive oil, then sprinkle with salt. Repeat with the remaining pieces of dough.

Bake, rotating the pans halfway through, until the crackers are blistered and golden brown, about 10 minutes. Transfer to a cooling rack and let cool completely. Bake the remaining crackers. The crackers will keep for 1 week in a paper bag. Reheat in a 300°F oven for 5 minutes to recrisp if necessary.

RED PEPPER & WALNUT CREMA

MAKES ABOUT 3 CUPS

My take on *m'hammara*—a traditional Middle Eastern spread—uses a little less garlic and oil than the classic version, making the smoky red peppers the star. If you omit the bread crumbs, you'll have a runnier mixture, more of a sauce than a spread, which can be used on grilled meats. Speaking of grilled meats: if you've got the grill rolling, try roasting those peppers over the coals instead of in the oven, which will add another layer of complexity to the finished spread.

4 red peppers

1½ cups walnuts, finely chopped

½ cup dry bread crumbs, toasted

3 tablespoons extra-virgin olive oil, plus more for garnish

1 tablespoon plus 1 teaspoon lemon juice

2 teaspoons kosher salt

2 teaspoons ground Aleppo pepper

1 teaspoon honey

½ clove garlic, crushed

¼ cup pine nuts, toasted, for garnish

Preheat the oven to 450°F. Put the red peppers on a rimmed baking sheet or in a cast-iron frying pan and transfer to the oven. Cook, rotating the peppers occasionally, until they are blistered and blackened on all sides, about 15 minutes. Transfer to a plastic bag (or a bowl covered with plastic wrap) and let steam until cool enough to handle. Peel, stem, and seed the peppers, then rinse under cold water and cut out and discard any membranes.

Put the roasted peppers in a food processor and add the walnuts, bread crumbs, olive oil, lemon juice, salt, Aleppo pepper, honey, and garlic and process until smooth. If the spread is very thick, add more olive oil. Taste and adjust the seasoning as needed, adding more salt, lemon juice, or Aleppo pepper.

Transfer to a bowl and garnish with a drizzle of olive oil and the pine nuts. Serve at room temperature with crackers (page 66), crudités, or toasts. The dip will keep, refrigerated, for up to 3 days.

CUCUMBER YOGURT CREAM

MAKES ABOUT 3 CUPS

This is my version of *tzatziki*, which I often serve in the summertime. I make a platter of Olive Oil Crackers (page 66), Red Pepper & Walnut Crema (page 69), and olives, but I have found that long after the crackers are gone guests will continue eating this, smeared on grilled vegetables and meat (it's especially good with lamb).

Full-fat Greek-style yogurt is a must here, or you can use a mixture of low-fat yogurt and sour cream. I find that the fat balances the yogurt's acidity and makes a thicker, creamier dip.

Using the large holes on a box grater, grate the cucumbers. Transfer to a colander and sprinkle with salt. Let stand for 10 minutes, then gently squeeze handfuls of grated cucumber to remove excess liquid and transfer to the bowl of a food processor.

Add the yogurt and olive oil and process to combine. Transfer to a serving bowl and stir in the mint. Season to taste with additional salt and pepper. Refrigerate until ready to serve. This is best eaten the same day it's made.

2 large cucumbers (about 1 pound), peeled and seeded	3 tablespoons extra-virgin olive oil
1 teaspoon kosher salt	2 tablespoons fresh mint, finely chopped
1½ cups full-fat Greek-style yogurt	Freshly ground black pepper

WHIPPED LARDO

MAKES ⅓ POUND

Lardo is pork back fat, cured with salt and herbs and then thinly sliced and served alongside other salumi. It originated in Colonnata, in Tuscany, where it was—and still is—cured in marble basins. Whipped lardo, in which the fat is not cured but rather ground, seasoned, and beaten until fluffy and spreadable, is another way to transform the rich back fat of the pig into something extraordinary. I have found that the back fat on pastured pork is softer than commercial pork, and the flavor is richer and sweeter. At Belcampo, we raise all of our pigs free-range not only because we believe it's the right thing to do, but also because the meat tastes infinitely better because of it. I always think that the proof of the pork is in the fat, and the fat of nonstressed pastured animals is sweet and clean tasting. This lardo can be spread on toasts or used as a rub on chicken or racks of lamb or goat.

⅓ pound pork back fat (or leaf lard)	About 1 tablespoon fresh rosemary leaves, minced
1 small clove garlic, minced	Kosher or sea salt
1 teaspoon sherry or red wine vinegar	Freshly ground black pepper

Cube the fat into ½-inch pieces, put on a rimmed baking sheet, and transfer to the freezer for 10 minutes.

Grind the fat through the smallest setting on a meat grinder. If you do not have a meat grinder, just hand-chop the fat with a chef's knife until the cubes are the size of almonds and then pulse in a food processor until the fat pieces are the size of kernels of wheat. Transfer the ground fat to a stand mixer fitted with the paddle attachment. Add the garlic and vinegar and mix on medium speed until the fat is smooth and soft, about 10 minutes. Increase the speed to high to add air to the mixture and whip the fat until it is light and fluffy, 5 minutes more. Season to taste with rosemary (you may not need all of it, so add it bit by bit), salt, and pepper.

Transfer the whipped lardo to a bowl and serve at room temperature with toast. It will keep for up to 3 weeks tightly wrapped in the refrigerator; let it come to room temperature before serving.

SNACKS, STARTERS & COCKTAILS

FARINATA

MAKES ONE 12-INCH *FARINATA*; SERVES 4 TO 6

This is one of my favorite starters, a thin, simple chickpea flour pancake with crispy edges. It's terrific with nothing more than some cracked pepper, but it can be enhanced with a topping of thinly sliced mortadella or strips of roasted red peppers. Though the batter can (and should) be made ahead, cook the *farinata* just before you plan to serve it—it's best fresh from the oven.

A rule of thumb: The simpler a recipe is, the better the ingredients need to be. In this dish, the flavor and consistency rely entirely on the quality of the chickpea flour. I suspect that many of the American chickpea flours are stored longer than the Italian ones, as I've found that when I make this dish with American chickpea flour, the pancakes taste a bit stale and drier than I'd like. I'm typically a proponent of sourcing ingredients locally, but in this case I suggest you seek out an Italian-brand chickpea flour online or in a specialty store.

This makes one 12-inch *farinata*. If you do not have a 12-inch cast-iron pan, you can use a smaller pan and make a couple of them. The important thing to note is that the batter should be no deeper than $1/4$ to $1/2$ inch in the pan or the *farinata* will not get crispy.

Combine the water and salt in a medium bowl and stir to dissolve the salt. Sift the chickpea flour into the salted water a little at a time, whisking to avoid lumps. Cover and let stand at room temperature for 3 hours.

Put a 12-inch cast-iron frying pan in the oven and preheat the oven to 500°F.

Skim any foam off the top of the chickpea batter and discard; the batter will be very liquid. Stir in 3 tablespoons of the oil.

When the oven is hot, remove the preheated pan, add the remaining 1 tablespoon oil, and tilt the pan so it coats the bottom. Pour in the batter and return the pan to the oven. Bake until the edges are deeply browned and a golden, blistered crust forms on top, about 10 minutes. Remove the pan from the oven and carefully remove the *farinata* with a spatula. Crack some black pepper over the *farinata* and arrange slices of mortadella on top, overlapping slightly. Cut the *farinata* into wedges and serve warm.

---

1 cup water

1 teaspoon kosher salt

1 cup chickpea flour

4 tablespoons extra-virgin olive oil

Freshly ground black pepper

¼ pound thinly sliced mortadella (optional)

PANZEROTTI

MAKES ABOUT 30 RAVIOLI;
SERVES 8 TO 10 AS A SNACK

These deep-fried ravioli, filled with ricotta and herbs, are a rich snack. Although they are fried, they can sit for up to 45 minutes without suffering, so I usually fry half of them about 15 minutes before guests arrive and the second batch a half hour into the party. This is another Sicilian favorite, and in Sicily you can find both sweet and savory versions. For savory fillings, I've experimented with adding grated hard cheese like Parmigiano-Reggiano as well as finely chopped arugula, green onions, and chives. For a dessert version, I sweeten the ricotta with confectioners' sugar and add a bit of lemon zest and cinnamon. If you've made your own ricotta (page 52), this is a great way to use it.

FOR THE FILLING

2 cups ricotta (page 52)

⅓ cup very finely chopped fresh parsley

1 egg

Kosher salt and freshly ground black pepper

FOR THE DOUGH

3¾ cups all-purpose flour

⅓ cup extra-virgin olive oil

¼ teaspoon kosher salt

1 cup lukewarm water

Canola or vegetable oil, for deep-frying

Prepare the ricotta filling: If your ricotta is very wet, line a fine-mesh sieve with a clean kitchen towel and drain the ricotta in it for 30 minutes. Depending on the ricotta you're using, draining may not be necessary; if the ricotta is more crumbly than creamy, skip this step. If you're not sure, draining can't hurt. Transfer the drained ricotta to a bowl, add the parsley and egg, and season with salt and pepper.

CONTINUED

To make the dough: In the bowl of a stand mixer fitted with a dough hook, combine the flour, olive oil, and salt. Add the water, then mix on low speed for 10 minutes until the dough comes together into a smooth, supple ball. Transfer the dough to a work surface, cover with a sheet of plastic wrap, and let rest for 10 minutes.

Divide the dough into three equal portions. Working with one strip of dough at a time, with a pasta roller or on a floured work surface with a

rolling pin, roll each into a 35-inch-long rectangle, 4 to 5 inches wide and $1/16$ inch thick. Lay one sheet of pasta flat on a lightly floured work surface and determine approximately where the halfway point is lengthwise. Spoon mounds of the filling, about 2 teaspoons each, onto half of the dough, leaving about 2 inches between the mounds. Using a pastry brush, brush the edge of the pasta sheet with water. Fold the pasta sheet over lengthwise to cover the filling. Press the pasta sheets together to seal the

edges around the filling, and press out any excess air. Use a knife to cut individual panzerotti and place them on a lightly floured baking sheet.

Heat 3 inches of oil in a high-sided heavy pot over high heat until the oil is hot but not smoking (it should register 375°F on a deep-frying thermometer). Line a baking sheet with paper towels. Fry the panzerotti a few at a time, in batches, until golden brown all over, about 3 minutes. With a spider or slotted spoon, transfer the fried panzerotti to the prepared baking sheet to drain, then sprinkle with salt and serve immediately. Repeat until all of the panzerotti have been fried, letting the oil return to temperature between each batch. Serve hot or at room temperature; the panzerotti can be fried up to 30 minutes before you plan to serve them.

FRIED MORTADELLA SANDWICHES

MAKES 4 SANDWICHES

I first tried fried mortadella sandwiches not in Italy but on a sweltering day in São Paulo, Brazil. I was on the second floor of a massive marketplace near the center of town in a food court that had six separate restaurants, each serving the same thing on the menu: sanduíche de mortadela. The sandwich was irresistable: soft bread crisped on the grill, about an inch of thin-cut griddled mortadella, and a layer of gooey cheese.

Frying the mortadella stacks is crucial to this recipe. The meat crisps irresistibly on its edges, and the small amount of fat that renders out of the mortadella is the perfect medium for toasting the bread, which absorbs the porky flavor. Though some specialty shops sell slices of massive mortadella (in Italy they are made up to a foot in diameter), for this recipe you want slices that are less than 5 inches in diameter. When serving the sandwiches as a starter, I cut them into quarters for an excellent handheld snack. Not surprisingly, the salty sandwiches are great with cocktails.

---

28 thin slices mortadella, no more than 5 inches in diameter

8 thin slices brioche or challah

8 slices provolone

Salted butter, for frying

Arrange the sliced mortadella into four even stacks of seven slices each. In a dry cast-iron or heavy frying pan over medium heat, fry the mortadella stacks, turning once, until sizzled and brown on both sides, about 6 minutes. Remove the pan from the heat.

Place each mortadella stack on a slice of bread and top with a slice of provolone and a second slice of bread to make a sandwich.

Return the pan to medium heat and add a few tablespoons of butter. Put the sandwiches in the pan and weight them down with a second, smaller cast-iron pan or other weight. Cook until golden brown on one side, about 3 minutes. Add more butter to the pan, flip the sandwiches, weight them down again, and cook until golden brown on the second side, about 3 minutes more. Remove from the pan, cut into halves or quarters, and serve hot.

FOCACCIA DI RECCO

MAKES 2 FOCACCIA; SERVES 8

The recipe for this thin, crispy cheese-filled focaccia hails from the coastal Italian region of Liguria. It looks spectacular and is a bit addictive—both qualities that make it a great starter for a dinner party. In the Ligurian bakeries that produce this, it's baked on massive hammered copper sheets in blazing pizza ovens, reaching blistered perfection in minutes. For a home version, I try to mimic the conditions by baking the focaccia on a thin baking sheet or directly on a pizza stone. It can be tricky to find Crescenza cheese, which is a mild cow's milk cheese that melts easily. If you can't find it, substitute queso blanco, tasting it for salt and adding some if necessary.

3 cups "00" flour

1 cup water

2 tablespoons extra-virgin olive oil, plus more for drizzling

1 tablespoon kosher salt

7 ounces Crescenza cheese

Flaky sea salt, such as Maldon

Combine the flour, water, olive oil, and kosher salt in the bowl of a stand mixer fitted with a dough hook. Mix on medium speed for about 10 minutes, until the ingredients come together into a smooth ball. Cover the bowl with plastic wrap and let stand for 15 minutes.

Preheat the oven to 500°F or as high as it will go. If using a pizza stone, preheat it along with the oven. Divide the dough into four even pieces and cover with plastic wrap or a clean kitchen towel to prevent the dough from drying out. Flour a work surface and rolling pin and, working with one piece of dough at a time, roll it into a paper-thin circle about 15 inches in diameter. Transfer the dough to a floured pizza peel (if using a pizza stone) or an unrimmed baking sheet. Dot the dough with half the cheese, then roll a second piece of dough the same size as the first and place over the top, crimping the edges of the two pieces of dough so they seal together. Drizzle the top with olive oil, sprinkle with sea salt, and transfer to the oven (if using a pizza stone, bake directly on the stone).

Bake until the focaccia is blistered and crackerlike on top (the bottom crust will remain softer but should have some dark brown spots), 5 to 7 minutes. Remove from the oven, let cool for 1 minute, then cut into wedges. Repeat with the remaining dough and cheese to make a second focaccia.

FRITTATINA D'ERBE

MAKES 2 THIN *FRITTATINA*; SERVES 8 AS A SNACK OR 4 FOR A LIGHT LUNCH

I learned to make these eggy disks not long after moving to Italy because I loved eating them. Though called frittata in Italy, they bear little resemble to any of the thick frittatas often served for brunch in the States. It's basically a very thin, herb-packed omelet that is cooked like a pancake—sizzled on one side until a golden crust forms, cooked over low heat until the top sets, then flipped with a wide spatula and browned on the other side.

Unlike a French-style omelet, these herby pancakes make amazing leftovers. I think the density of the herbs and the touch of cheese keeps them tasting fresh and delicious a day or two after they're made, and in Italy they're often cut into wedges, slathered with aioli, and eaten as a sandwich filling. I usually serve them as finger food, cut into strips or wedges. The "party" version of this that I saw occasionally in Italy is a stack of omelets, each flavored with a different herb or leftover cooked vegetable, glued together with mayonnaise. The end result looks like a savory layer cake and is definitely spectacular, although difficult to eat.

In addition to herbs, I'll also use leftover cooked vegetables in my *frittatina*. My favorites are zucchini combined with fresh mint or finely chopped, braised or roasted fennel mixed with minced parsley. For a splash of color, finely chopped roasted red peppers are great, especially when combined with fresh basil.

CONTINUED

6 eggs

½ cup finely grated Parmigiano-Reggiano cheese

½ cup fresh parsley, chopped

2 tablespoons mixed minced fresh thyme, sage, and oregano

4 tablespoons (½ stick) salted butter

2 tablespoons extra-virgin olive oil

In a medium bowl, whisk together the eggs, Parmigiano-Reggiano, and herbs. Heat a 9-inch cast-iron or nonstick pan over high heat and add 1 tablespoon of the butter and 1 tablespoon of the oil. When the butter has melted, add half of the egg mixture. Cook for 2 minutes. Using a spatula, gently lift the edges so the uncooked egg mixture on the top of the *frittatina* flows into the pan.

Lower the heat to the lowest setting, cover, and cook until the *frittatina* is firm on top, about 5 minutes. With a large spatula, lift the *frittatina* out of the pan and flip top side down onto a plate or pot lid. Add another tablespoon of the butter to the pan, then slide the *frittatina* back into the pan, top side down. Increase the heat to high and cook until deep golden brown on the second side, about 1 minute. Transfer to a plate or cutting board and let cool to room temperature, then cut into wedges. Repeat with the remaining egg mixture, butter, and oil to make a second *frittatina*. The *frittatina* will keep, refrigerated, for several days.

ROASTED PEPPERS WITH SALTED FISH

SERVES 6

This simple snack is traditional in northern Italy. The intense sweetness of roasted peppers is countered by the brininess of the anchovies. The little "rollmops," which resemble the British snack of that name, typically made with pickled herring, are beautiful and delicious. Use the best oil you have for drizzling on top.

16 salt-cured anchovies	Extra-virgin olive oil, for drizzling
8 red peppers	

Preheat the oven to 450°F and line a plate with paper towels. Put the anchovies in a bowl and cover with cold water. Let soak for 30 minutes, then gut, pull the anchovy fillets from the bones, and transfer the fillets to the prepared plate.

Put the peppers on a rimmed baking sheet and transfer to the oven. Cook, rotating the peppers occasionally, until they are blistered and blackened on all sides, about 15 minutes. Transfer to a plastic bag (or to a bowl covered with plastic wrap) and let stand until cool enough to handle.

Peel, stem, and seed the peppers, then rinse under cold water and discard any membranes. Cut each pepper into four strips, then top each strip with one of the anchovy fillets. Roll the pepper around the anchovy fillet, using a toothpick to secure it. Transfer the finished rolls to a serving plate and drizzle with olive oil.

PICKLED BEETS (& PINK PICKLED EGGS)

MAKES ABOUT 4 CUPS

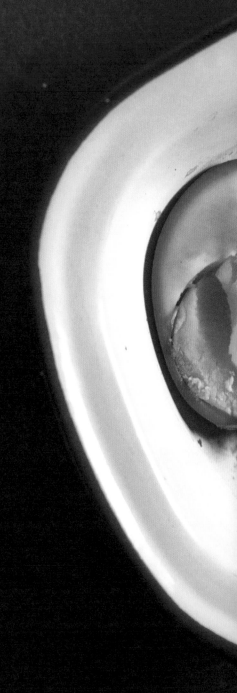

I keep these pickles in my fridge pretty much all winter long and serve them anytime I am cooking a meat-heavy meal that benefits from a bright, acidic starter. They're quick to make and are ready to eat in a day, so they don't require the preplanning that most vegetable pickles do. For a starter or a light lunch, you can also add peeled hard-boiled eggs to the brine and let them pickle for a day or two alongside the beets (no longer, or they develop the texture of a rubber bouncy ball). If you use red beets, the egg whites turn a brilliant fuchsia.

---

5 medium red or golden beets

2 cups apple cider vinegar

2 cups water

¼ cup sugar

2 tablespoons kosher salt

6 hard-boiled eggs (optional)

Put the beets in a medium saucepan and add water to cover. Bring to a boil over high heat and boil until the beets are tender but not mushy, 30 to 45 minutes. Drain, rinse with cool water, peel, and cut into 1-inch cubes.

Add the vinegar, water, sugar, and salt to the now-empty saucepan and bring to a boil, stirring to dissolve the sugar and salt. Remove from the heat.

Put the beets in a heatproof jar with a lid and pour the brine over. Peel the hard-boiled eggs and add them to the brine along with the beets. Let cool, then cover and transfer to the refrigerator. The beets are ready in a day but will keep, refrigerated, for up to 6 weeks; the eggs should be eaten within a day or two.

SCACCIA RAGUSANO

MAKES ONE 12-INCH *SCACCIA*; SERVES 6 TO 8

If lasagna and focaccia had a baby, its name would be *scaccia Ragusano*. This folded bread bakes into a crusty loaf, while the interior layers of dough, soaked in tomato sauce and layered with cheese, meld together like a layered lasagna. At my workplace in Ragusa, Sicily, our days were structured to allow for a long break midday to go home and eat. On the hottest summer days, this break stretched to four hours, and on a few memorable occasions, some of my colleagues and I would drive down to the beach and spend a few hours in the water, swimming and sometimes foraging for sea urchins in the shallow water. *Scaccia* is sold everywhere in Ragusa, so we would grab a few big ones and share them for lunch on the beach. That memory—of salt and sun and the taste of the *scaccia*—is something indelible in my mind.

The traditional cheese used to make this, Ragusano, is named after this town. It's a salty aged provolone that melts very well. Ragusano was created to withstand aging in conditions where the temperature regularly climbs above 100°F in the summer, the natural climate of its region of origin. The giant rectangular cheeses are almost 3 feet long; to age, they are hung from hemp ropes in natural caves. The special salty and slightly musky flavor of that cheese definitely adds something to the *scaccia*, but because it's difficult to find outside of Sicily, you can substitute any well-aged provolone.

1 cup warm water	3 cloves garlic, minced
¼ teaspoon instant dry yeast	1 small bunch basil
1¼ cups "OO" flour	10 ounces aged provolone, grated
1¼ cups semolina flour	Freshly ground black pepper
½ teaspoon kosher salt	Olive oil, for drizzling
1 (28-ounce) can crushed tomatoes	

Put the water in the bowl of a stand mixer fitted with the dough hook attachment. Sprinkle the yeast into the water and let stand until foamy, about 5 minutes.

Add the flours and salt and turn the mixer on low. Mix until the dough comes together into a smooth ball, 10 to 12 minutes. Transfer to a lightly oiled bowl, cover with a clean kitchen towel, and let rest in a warm place until doubled in size, about 1 hour.

While the dough rises, combine the crushed tomatoes, garlic, and a few sprigs of basil in a medium saucepan. Bring to a simmer over medium-high heat and simmer for 10 minutes, stirring occasionally. Season lightly to taste with salt (the cheese is salty, so go light). Transfer to a bowl and let cool; remove and discard the basil sprigs.

Preheat the oven to 450°F and line a baking sheet with parchment paper. Gently punch down the dough and transfer to a lightly floured work surface. Dust the dough with flour and, with a lightly

floured rolling pin, roll into a large rectangle 11 by 17 inches and about 1/16 inch thick. Arrange the dough so that the long sides are parallel to you. Spread 1 cup of tomato sauce over the dough in a thin layer, spreading all the way to the edges, and sprinkle with 1½ cups of cheese; season with salt and pepper. Lay a few basil leaves across the dough.

Fold the left third of the dough toward the center, spread the top with ¼ cup sauce, and sprinkle with some of the remaining cheese; season with salt and pepper and lay a few more basil leaves on top. Fold the right third over the center to meet the left edge, and repeat with sauce, cheese, salt, pepper, and basil. Fold in the top and bottom of the dough so they meet in center, spread the top with the

remaining sauce and cheese, season with salt and pepper, and add a few more leaves of basil. Fold the top half over the bottom half, like closing a book, and transfer to the prepared baking sheet. Drizzle olive oil over the top and sprinkle with salt.

Bake for 10 minutes, then lower the oven temperature to 400°F and continue baking until deep golden brown, 45 to 50 minutes. Let cool for at least 10 minutes, then cut into thin slices.

SMALL FISH FRY

SERVES 4 TO 6

This is my riff on an Italian street food favorite: paper cones of salty fried small fish served with a dollop of creamy aioli and a wedge of lemon. For me, this is the highest and best use for small fish like smelt and anchovies because the fish don't need to be gutted, beheaded, or scaled, and because tiny crispy fish are really good to eat. This is a great party food—for a fun presentation, serve the fried fish in cones made from newspaper.

1 pound (about 20) whole small fish, such as smelt or anchovies	1 tablespoon fine sea salt
	Canola oil, for frying
1 cup "OO" flour	Lemon wedges, for serving
	Aioli (page 17), for serving

Rinse the fish in cold water and drain on paper towels. In a shallow baking dish (such as a pie plate), combine the flour and salt.

Preheat the oven to 200°F and line a baking sheet with paper towels. Add a 2-inch depth of canola oil to a high-sided heavy pot and set over high heat. Dredge the fish in the flour, turning to coat on all sides. When the oil registers 365°F on a deep-frying thermometer, add some of the fish and fry until they curl and turn deep golden brown, about 4 minutes. Remove from the oil with a spider or slotted spoon and transfer to the prepared baking sheet to drain, then put the sheet in the oven to keep warm while you fry the remaining fish, allowing the oil to return to 365°F between each batch.

When all of the fish have been fried, transfer to newspaper cones or a platter and season to taste with additional salt. Serve with lemon wedges and a bowl of aioli.

BRIGHT & FRESH TOMATO SOUP

SERVES 4

Like many of us, I have nostalgia for the canned tomato soup my mom used to serve me when I was a kid. I began making this soup at the end of a long day of tomato canning, when I was left with more tomato puree than jars to can it in. (I also learned to make ketchup that day.) Now I regularly make it from fresh tomatoes or from my canned tomato puree. Because the ingredients in this soup are few, if you opt for store-bought rather than homemade tomato puree, get the best quality you can find.

---

4 cups homemade tomato passato (page 24) or store-bought tomato puree

2 cups Bone Broth (page 20)

1 (3 by 1-inch) Parmigiano-Reggiano rind

Kosher salt and freshly ground black pepper

Extra-virgin olive oil, for drizzling

Combine the tomato puree, bone broth, and rind in a large saucepan. Bring to a boil over medium-high heat, then lower the heat so the liquid is simmering very gently, and simmer for 1 hour. Remove the rind and season to taste with salt and pepper. Ladle the soup into warmed bowls and drizzle with olive oil. Serve hot.

COCKTAILS

PEACH SHRUB

MAKES ABOUT 3 CUPS

Shrubs are vinegar-based fruit syrups that can either be used as a juice concentrate (mixed with soda water) or mixed into cocktails to complement and enhance spirits. This is one of my favorite versions, as the natural pulpiness of the peaches makes the final product really thick and luscious. This shrub pairs well with most white spirits, from moonshine to light rum. For a simple shrub-based cocktail, mix equal parts spirit, shrub, and soda water with a dash of bitters.

4 ripe peaches (about 1 pound), peeled, pitted, and cut into chunks

1 cup sugar

¾ cup apple cider vinegar

Put the peach chunks in a bowl and, with a potato masher or your fingers, mash into a chunky paste. You should have 1½ cups mashed peaches. Mix the sugar into the peaches. Don't be afraid to be rough with it; the solids are later discarded, so you want to extract as much juice and pulp as possible. Cover the bowl with plastic wrap and refrigerate overnight.

Press the peach mixture through a fine-mesh sieve into a clean bowl, pressing hard on the solids to extract as much juice and pulp as possible. Discard any pulp trapped by the sieve. Whisk in the vinegar, then transfer to a mason jar or bottle with a tight-fitting lid and refrigerate for 5 days, shaking periodically to dissolve the sugar. The shrub will keep, refrigerated, for up to 3 months.

BITTERS

Homemade bitters are a great way to shape the personality of a cocktail. There are countless varieties commercially available now, but I still like making my own. Bitters last indefinitely; packaged into small dropper bottles, they're a nice gift. To make the orange version, you'll need quassia bark, the bark of a large deciduous tree, which adds a distinct bitterness to the liquid. It can be sourced online.

ORANGE BITTERS

MAKES 2 CUPS

4 navel oranges	1 tablespoon caraway seeds
1 cup high-proof rum	1½ teaspoons whole cloves
1 cup high-proof bourbon	2 whole star anise
1 tablespoon quassia bark	½ teaspoon anise seed

Preheat the oven to 350°F. With a vegetable peeler, remove the peels from the oranges in long strips and put on a baking sheet (reserve the peeled fruit for another use). Bake until the peels are brittle and dry, about 30 minutes. Let cool, then transfer to a quart-size jar with a tight-fitting lid.

Add the rum, bourbon, quassia bark, caraway seeds, cloves, star anise, and anise seed, stir well to combine, then cover and let stand at room temperature for 1 month.

After a month, strain the mixture into a clean jar, discarding the solids. The bitters will keep in a cool, dark place indefinitely; they do not need to be refrigerated.

RHUBARB BITTERS

MAKES 2 CUPS

2 navel oranges	1 ounce agave nectar
1 lemon	¾ pound rhubarb, cut into 2-inch lengths
1½ cups high-proof grain alcohol, such as Everclear	1 cinnamon stick
¾ cup water	

Preheat the oven to 350°F. With a vegetable peeler, remove the peels from the oranges and the lemon in long strips and put on a baking sheet (reserve the peeled fruit for another use). Bake until the peels are brittle and dry, about 30 minutes. Let cool, then transfer to a quart-size jar with a tight-fitting lid.

Add the alcohol, water, and agave nectar and stir well to combine, then add the rhubarb pieces and cinnamon stick, cover, and let stand at room temperature for 1 month.

After a month, strain the mixture into a clean jar, discarding the solids. The bitters will keep in a cool, dark place indefinitely; they do not need to be refrigerated.

TI PUNCH

SERVES 8

Ti (pronounced "tea") punch is a restrained version of a daiquiri that's one of my favorite summertime drinks. It retains a lot of intensity while still having that refreshing citrus-booze balance and is a great way to highlight any light rum. If you want, you can use a mix of white and gold rum to give the cocktail more depth.

---

3 cups agricole rum	Ice cubes
½ cup simple syrup	Lime wedges, for garnish
½ cup freshly squeezed lime juice	

In a quart-size mason jar, stir together the rum, simple syrup, and lime juice. Refrigerate until ready to serve (the mixture will keep for 1 day in the refrigerator).

Pour ½ cup of the mixture into a rocks glass with one large cube of ice. Stir and garnish with a lime wedge.

LIGURIAN SANGRIA

SERVES 6

This is a light summer drink that pairs well with salty starters, particularly egg- and aioli-based bites. I love the way this drink looks, luminescent and pink, and it's an easy one to make ahead, as it holds up well in the fridge—top with Champagne or sparkling water just before serving. I first tasted this on a terrace in Italy at a summer party, where it was described as "peaches in wine." I later learned it's a traditional summer drink all along the northern Italian coast. If you want a lower-alcohol version, just omit the rum.

---

2 large peaches, peeled and pitted	1 bottle (750 ml) cold dry white wine
Juice of 1 lime	½ cup light rum
1 tablespoon sugar	Champagne or sparkling wine (optional)

Combine the peaches, lime juice, and sugar in the bowl of a food processor and process until smooth. Transfer to a pitcher and top with the wine and rum. The sangria can be drunk right away or refrigerated until ready to serve; stir before serving, as the peach solids will sink. To serve, pour into wineglasses and, if desired, top with a float of Champagne.

BATCHED BOULEVARDIER

SERVES 8

This cocktail's inherent bitterness and complexity mandates that it's a sipping drink, something to nurse over a long conversation. Perfect for winter entertaining, it has a deep, complex flavor that belies its simplicity. Because it's an all-spirit mixture, it can be made ahead and stored, refrigerated, for many months.

1¼ cups rye whiskey	Ice
1 cup Campari	Orange twist, for garnish
1 cup sweet vermouth	

In a quart-size mason jar, stir together the whiskey, Campari, and vermouth. Store in the refrigerator until ready to serve. To serve, pour 3 ounces into an ice-filled shaker or mixing glass and stir for 30 seconds. Strain into a cocktail glass and garnish with an orange twist.

VERMOUTH COCKTAIL

SERVES 1

I often kick off a dinner party by serving my guests a glass of sweet or dry vermouth on ice with an orange twist. I like to think of vermouth as a premixed cocktail—it has bitterness, sweetness, and acid and is great sipped all by its lonesome or topped with a bit of sparkling wine or water. Because vermouth is low in alcohol (about the same amount as wine), you can enjoy a cocktail or two without feeling the effects too tremendously.

If you want to fancy things up, the recipe below is a blend of vermouths and inky crème de cassis that's incredibly refreshing.

1½ ounces Cocchi Americano	¾ ounce crème de cassis
1½ ounces dry white vermouth	Ice cube
	Soda water

Combine the Cocchi, vermouth, and crème de cassis in a rocks glass and stir to combine. Add a large ice cube and top with a float of soda water.

BOURBON OLD FASHIONED

SERVES 1

Though this drink is fairly ubiquitous, I am including a recipe for it here to remind home cooks how easy, impressive, and delicious this cocktail is. One reason I like it for parties is that it doesn't require simple syrup, which, while easy enough to make, is sometimes the deal-breaking extra step. This drink is a great way to showcase an amazing bourbon, so break out the good stuff here.

4 dashes orange bitters (page 97)

2 Demerara sugar cubes or 1 teaspoon Demerara sugar

2 orange wheels

Ice cube

2 ounces bourbon or rye whiskey

In an old fashioned glass, muddle the bitters, sugar, and 1 orange wheel. Remove the orange from the glass, add one large ice cube, and pour the bourbon over. Garnish with a fresh orange wheel.

VARIATIONS

I've had fun making versions of this cocktail, swapping in a different spirit for the bourbon and experimenting with different types of bitters, sugars, and garnishes. Here are a few of my favorite variations—we can call them "new fashioneds."

GRAPPA NEW FASHIONED

SERVES 1

Dandelion and burdock are a combination that has been popular in Britain since the 1300s, when beverages made with the two ingredients were said to have medicinal properties. A few dashes of dandelion and burdock bitters contribute an herbaceous bitterness to the drink; you can purchase it—and dozens of other unusual bitters—online at themeadow.com.

2 or 3 dashes dandelion and burdock bitters	Ice cube
1 Demerara sugar cube or ½ teaspoon Demerara sugar	2 ounces 5-year-aged grappa
	Lemon twist, for garnish

In an old fashioned glass, muddle the bitters and sugar. Add one large ice cube to the glass and pour the grappa over. Garnish with a lemon twist.

COGNAC-WALNUT NEW FASHIONED

SERVES 1

This is a super elegant twist on an old-fashioned—lots of complex flavors that really fill your palate. The dark nuttiness pairs especially well with holiday favorites. I also love this as a drink to serve towards the end of dinner.

2 or 3 dashes black walnut bitters	Ice cube
1 Demerara sugar cube or ½ teaspoon Demerara sugar	2 ounces Cognac
	Club soda
	Orange twist, for garnish

In an old fashioned glass, muddle the bitters and sugar. Add one large ice cube to the glass and pour the Cognac over. Top with a splash of club soda and garnish with an orange twist.

My approach to entertaining

I was twelve years old and my family had just moved to Palo Alto, California, from Eugene, Oregon. We were settling into a new house in a new town and my parents were having a small Thanksgiving with a few of their new friends—maybe eight people total. My mom slid the turkey into the oven but a few hours later the stove in our rented house went on the fritz, and the turkey skin darkened too quickly, though the inside was still raw. My mom melted down, undoubtedly due to the stress of both the meal and the recent move.

I had always liked to help her cook, but that day I climbed into the driver's seat: I made the potatoes, I finished the turkey, I cooked the carrots and the green beans. She recovered in time to make the creamed pearl onions and together we baked the pies. It's a Thanksgiving division of labor we have maintained since. That day, I discovered that I loved not only cooking, but also the feeling of accomplishment that comes with pulling something off to the delight and pleasure of others.

I still love the challenge of preparing a meal, with many elements coming together like a piece of music, a performance. It's the same thing I love about being an entrepreneur and a parent: I'm forced to think on my feet, to step back and figure out solutions for making an evening seamless and fun. As I've gotten older and developed a passion for eating good food, gardening, and cooking, my family dinners have become more elaborate and interesting, but my entertaining philosophy—to serve a good meal without stress—remains the same.

My time in Italy helped mature an approach to entertaining and sharing meals that built on my natural enthusiasm for execution and organization, tempered by the

Italians' ingrained sense of ease and enjoyment. Living in Italy, I participated in so many family meals where the cook enjoyed it alongside the guests, with much of the work done ahead. My former mother-in-law, Irene Ciravegna, set a fine example. When my then-husband and I would come for Sunday dinner, we'd be greeted by a platter of whole fennel, a bowl of *carne cruda*, and a wedge of pecorino, with a plate of fresh olive oil alongside. We would spend the first half hour snacking, cutting the fennel into rounds, dipping it into the oil, and dabbing it with salt, while she would finish pulling things out of the oven and eventually join us. It felt easy and effortless.

I now do the same, setting out one or two things that my guests can start on immediately when they arrive: a whole salami, ready to slice, a platter of soft-boiled eggs topped with anchovy fillets, and a bowl of radishes or cherry tomatoes. Those snacks, and a drink in everyone's hand, gives me a chance to finish any last-minute cooking.

For a larger party of more than eight people, I like to plate a first course and serve the second course family-style, and I usually move any starters to the table so that people can keep munching. I find that plating that first dish makes it easier for people to dive in and keeps conversation flowing, and by the time we get the family-style main course, everyone has become friendly and is happy to pass the platters and serve themselves and others. For a smaller party, I do the whole dinner family-style, usually in two courses. Even if the dinner is just two courses, serving them sequentially slows you down and encourages your guests to relax into the dinner.

For any type of group entertaining indoors, I focus on dishes that can be prepared in advance. Unless I am outside at a grill, I avoid serving steak to a group of more than four; it requires too much last-minute cooking to do properly. A few sides or salads, always served family-style, fill things out. I keep dessert simple: a plate of sliced Panforte (page 253) or cookies alongside fruit and some chunks of nice old cheese; chocolate bars broken into pieces, or a make-ahead favorite like Jam Tartlets (page 275) or Baba au Rhum (page 256). If I'm entertaining outdoors, the same rules apply: I use the grill to cook a starter, the main course, and one side dish, then round out the meal with cold vegetable salads.

Throwing the best party

I throw a lot of parties, both at my home in Oakland and at the Belcampo farm up near the Oregon border. Cooking for friends and family is one of my favorite things to do. While no two parties are alike, owing to the event, the season, and the guests, I've developed strategies that allow me to pull it off seamlessly and actually enjoy each one.

Get comfortable: A dinner party is not the time to stress yourself out. Just as the comfort of your guests is important, so, too, is your own comfort. Plan a menu that you can execute with a minimum of stress.

Cook within your limits: If you have a complex recipe you've been dreaming of making but that might be a stretch for you, make it a few times first when the stakes are low, perfecting your technique before serving it to guests. In general, I stick to a tried-and-true party repertoire, because no matter how epic the food is, if the host is stressed, it's not going to be a great party.

Make it ahead: In keeping with this idea, I usually try to make the majority of the menu ahead of time. My best parties are invariably the ones where the only thing I am making when the guests arrive is a salad; the main course is usually something that just needs to be warmed and served, like involtini (page 224) or braised rabbit (page 208). Knowing that I don't have any major cooking tasks left when my guests arrive helps me relax and enjoy myself, which in turn allows me to tend to the comfort of my guests.

The importance of drinks: I like to have at least two drink options available for guests the second they walk through the door. I usually offer a batched cocktail (no cocktail mixing to order, please!) and either beer, cider, or wine. Depending on the crowd, I might also set out a fruit shrub and some sparkling water so guests can make their own spritzers.

Abundance: I also am a big believer in abundance—when friends arrive, I usually have at least three and up to six snacks for them to eat immediately, like Panzerotti (page 74), Torta di Verdure (page 155), or Chickpea Torte (page 166) cut into chunks. If you're short on time, a big piece of cheese and a bowl of great olives or almonds can work in a pinch, in which case I try to at least go to the effort of grilling some bread in a cast-iron pan, serving it with lots of good butter and some flaky salt.

Delegate: There is always someone at every party who will ask if he or she can help, so I usually set aside a job or two that is simple but helpful: grating cheese, lighting candles, or topping off drinks while I finish the preparations for the main course.

Sweet ending: Though I do not have a huge sweet tooth, many of my guests do, and toward the end of the evening I find that guests love to linger and talk. I always like to serve a little something to conclude the evening. My default is to break up a couple of good chocolate bars and pile them on a plate with some dates or other dried fruit, or serve squares of homemade nougat (page 264). If the meal was especially simple, I might make a more elaborate dessert, but always something that can be done in advance and simply sliced and served. It's also a great time to serve an interesting spirit—a thimble of your best bourbon or aged rum. This is when the best conversations happen.

TAKE A SEAT

PASTA, RAGU, RISOTTO & EGGS

VEGETABLES

FISH & MEAT

The food I make at home is rustic, and the recipes are flexible; many can be made ahead and reheated or hold well as you wait for guests to arrive or kids to sit down for dinner.

If I know I want to serve meat, I plan my dinner menu starting at the butcher shop and then round it out at the grocery store or the farmers' market. If I'm planning a vegetable-centric meal, I might reverse that, starting my shopping at the market. I find my food is best when the menu is inspired by whatever meat, fish, or vegetables look the most appealing. If you get stuck on making a particular dish, and then find that you're not able to get your hands on excellent ingredients, the finished dish is not going to be great, no matter how wonderful the recipe. It's about balance, too. If I'm planning to serve a rich starter, I might aim to make the main course a little lighter, or vice versa. And like most cooks, I find that the seasons dictate what I want to eat— more braises and roasts in winter, more vegetables and grilled meat in summer.

From a health perspective, I try to eat offal once a week, mostly iron-rich liver and heart, and to eat lesser cuts that require longer cooking frequently, too. I like the flavor of these cuts and it resonates with my personal and professional commitment to eat more than just the prime cuts of the animal. I am fortunate that my daughter, Viola, is an exuberant carnivore (she teethed on drumsticks and goat chops, which probably helped), but I always prepare a simple dish of durum pasta with butter and peas when I have kids coming over for dinner. That said, we don't eat *only* meat. My time in Italy gave me an appreciation for pasta, of course, as well as vegetable tarts and egg-centric main courses. When crab season begins or salmon starts running, I can't resist eating them as often as possible. And I'm a Northern California cook, after all, so vegetables are a constant.

PASTA, RAGU, RISOTTO & EGGS

EGGS POACHED IN TOMATO

SERVES 4

If you can tomatoes in the fall, this dish is a natural day-after meal. It's also a great way to use that extra jar of tomato puree lingering in the fridge after making a stew or ragu. It's an excellent brunch dish—you can prepare the tomato sauce ahead of time, then warm it and poach the eggs. Keep an eye on the eggs when poaching, taking care not to overcook them; it's such a treat when the soft yolks ooze into the tomato sauce. Note that the eggs will continue to cook even after the dish has been pulled from the heat, so I cook them only until the whites are set but the yolks are still quite runny, counting on some carryover cooking. Serve this with crusty bread alongside for sopping up the juices or spoon it over cooked farro for a filling main course. Since tomatoes can vary so much in sweetness, be sure to taste the pulp after you've cooked it down to adjust for salt—you may need a little more than you think if you've gotten very ripe, sweet tomatoes.

8 small ripe tomatoes, such as Early Girls or Romas

1 tablespoon extra-virgin olive oil

¼ cup Sofritto (page 17)

Kosher salt

4 eggs

1 cup grated Parmigiano-Reggiano cheese

Baguette or buttered toast, for serving

Using the large holes on a box grater, coarsely grate the tomatoes into a medium bowl, discarding the skins.

In an 8-inch cast-iron frying pan, heat the olive oil over medium-high heat. Add the sofritto and fry for 1 minute, then stir in the tomato pulp, turn the heat down to low, and cook, stirring occasionally, until the sauce has thickened. Season to taste with salt.

Make four wells in the tomato sauce and crack an egg into each. Sprinkle with the Parmigiano-Reggiano, cover, and cook for 2 minutes, until the whites are set but the yolks are still quite runny, then remove the pan from the heat and let stand for 10 minutes; the eggs will finish cooking in the residual heat. Serve hot, accompanied by a chunk of baguette or some buttered toast.

ASPARAGUS WITH FRIED EGGS & AIOLI

SERVES 4

This recipe evolved from my experiences gathering and cooking wild asparagus for Pasquetta back when I lived in Sicily. Pasquetta is a celebration that takes place the Monday after Easter, when Italians go for a hike and a picnic—a nice antidote to Sunday's marathon Easter dinner.

We would head out in the morning and gather wild asparagus for a few hours. We'd have our picnic lunch, make a campfire, then play cards and hang out all afternoon. When the fire was just a bed of coals, we'd put a cast-iron pan over the embers and fry the asparagus with a few duck eggs for dinner.

I recommend using skinny spears of asparagus in this recipe, mostly out of nostalgia for the wild asparagus I used to gather back in the day. However, this recipe will work just as well with thick asparagus; just be sure to cut off the woody bases of the stalks. The aioli is optional—I add it if I am making this dish for company. If it's a Wednesday-night dinner for me and my daughter, Viola, I'll usually do just the asparagus and eggs. Naturally, this is also a great brunch dish.

Preheat the oven to 450°F. Put the asparagus in a 12-inch cast-iron skillet, piling them up. Drizzle with ¼ cup of the olive oil and sprinkle with kosher salt. Use your hands to toss so all the spears are coated in oil. Transfer to the oven and roast for 10 to 15 minutes, tossing halfway through, until the spears are tender and the tips crisp. Remove from the oven and transfer to a platter.

Meanwhile, fry the eggs. Heat the remaining 2 tablespoons oil in a large frying pan over medium-high heat. When the oil is hot, crack the eggs into the pan and fry until the whites are set but the yolks are still runny, about 3 minutes. Slide the eggs on top of the asparagus and sprinkle with some flaky salt and ground pepper. Serve immediately, accompanied by the aioli, if using.

---

40 stalks (about 2 bunches) thin asparagus, ends trimmed

¼ cup plus 2 tablespoons extra-virgin olive oil

2 teaspoons kosher salt

4 eggs

Flaky salt, such as Maldon, and freshly ground black pepper

½ cup Aioli (page 17), (optional), for serving

MALTAGLIATI

MAKES ABOUT 12 OUNCES; SERVES 4 TO 6

For novice fresh pasta makers, maltagliati—Italian for "badly cut"—is the perfect gateway pasta: you make a dough from scratch and roll it thinly, essential pasta-making skills, but then the noodles can be roughly cut any which way and it still turns out okay. Maltagliati are equally good when sauced with either a meaty ragu or some fresh basil pesto.

2¼ cups "00" flour	1½ teaspoons extra-virgin olive oil
1½ teaspoons kosher salt	½ cup water
6 egg yolks	Semolina flour, for dusting

In a medium bowl, whisk together the flour and salt, then pour the flour onto a clean, dry work surface and form into a mound. Make a well in the center of the mound and add the yolks and olive oil to the well. Using a fork, gently beat the eggs, then begin incorporating some flour from the walls of the mound. Add the water to the egg yolks and continue slowly incorporating the flour with the fork until the dough begins to come together into a ball.

Knead the dough until it forms a smooth, supple ball, about 15 minutes, during which time the dough will go from sticky and rough to smooth and elastic; avoid adding any additional flour while kneading, if possible. Wrap the dough tightly in plastic wrap and let rest at room temperature for at least 30 minutes. (The dough can be refrigerated overnight. Remove from the refrigerator and let come to room temperature before rolling.)

Dust two rimmed sheet pans with semolina flour. Cut the ball of dough into thirds. Working with one ball of dough at a time (keeping the other two covered with a clean kitchen towel or sheet of plastic wrap to prevent them from drying out), roll it with a rolling pin so it will fit through the widest setting of an electric or hand cranked pasta machine. Pass it through the widest setting of the pasta machine twice, then pass it through the next two settings twice, at which point the dough should be twice as long as when you began.

Fold the strip of dough over onto itself into a rectangle about 6 inches wide, then gently press the layers together with the rolling pin. Pass this rectangle through the widest setting of the pasta machine again, then pass through each subsequent setting until the dough is ⅛ to ¹⁄₁₆ inch thick, using your hands to support—but not pull—the dough as it passes through the machine.

If you are rolling the dough by hand, divide the dough into thirds and roll each ball into a 4-inch disk with a rolling pin. Let the disks rest a few minutes (which lets the dough relax and makes it easier to roll it thin) and roll again to double its diameter. Let rest and roll a third time until you get the dough down to ⅛ to ¹⁄₁₆ inch thick.

Cut the pasta sheets into rectangles approximately 12 inches long, dust with semolina flour, and place on the baking sheets in stacks of four or five, dusting with semolina between each layer. Let stand for 10 minutes, until the sheets are slightly dried. Cut the stacks into long strips, about 2 inches wide, then cut or tear the strips into 2-inch squares. Return to the semolina-dusted baking sheets.

Bring a large pot of water to a boil and salt it. When the water is at a rolling boil, add a handful of semolina flour to the water, then add the pasta and cook until the sheets float and are just tender, 1 to 2 minutes. Drain, reserving some of the starchy cooking water, and toss with your choice of sauce, such as Bird & Bunny Ragu (page 132), Beef & Pork Ragu (page 128), or butter and grated Parmigiano-Reggiano cheese.

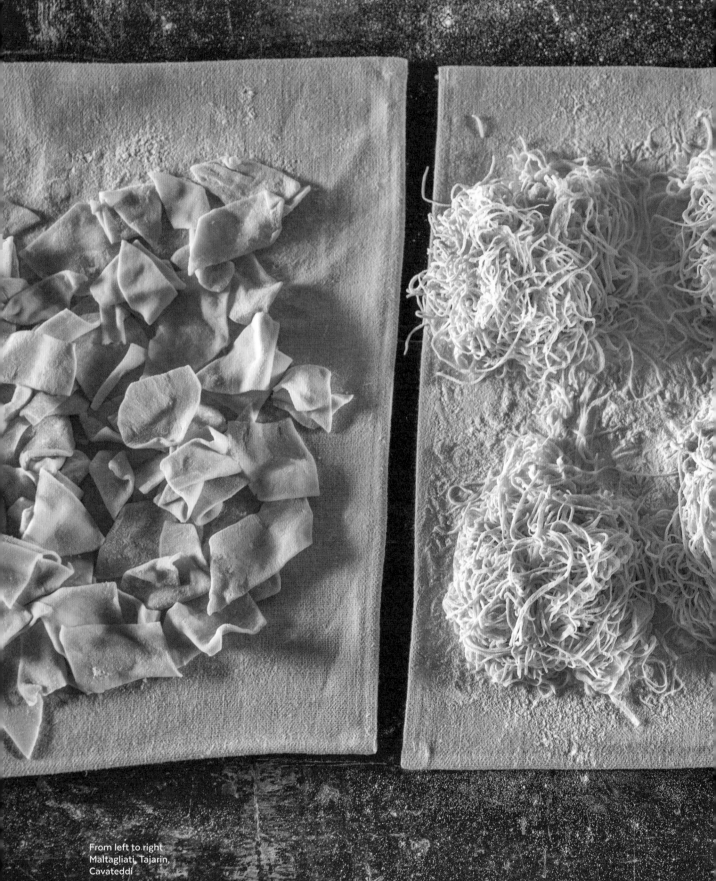

From left to right:
Maltagliati, Tajarin,
Cavateddi

CAVATEDDI

MAKES ABOUT 12 OUNCES; SERVES 4 TO 6

This is a Sicilian version of gnocchi made with a basic semolina flour and water dough. I first ate cavateddi when I was working in Sicily with a group of cheese makers. Many farm dinners featured a big plate of these, dressed with a light tomato sauce and a healthy amount of crumbled spicy pork sausage, covered with a drift of the local aged pecorino. That image of the plate of cavateddi swimming in sauce and a large plastic jug of fresh wine beside it is burned in my brain, forever associated with great, great nights.

Make sure you cook the cavateddi for a minute or two after they've risen to the top of the boiling water before you drain them, or they will be too doughy and leaden. The cooked pasta also benefits from being briefly cooked in sauce just before serving; they act as sponges for a flavorful ragu.

¾ cup warm water	1 cup all-purpose flour
1 tablespoon kosher salt	1 tablespoon extra-virgin olive oil
1 cup semolina flour, plus more for sprinkling	

In a measuring cup, combine the water and salt and stir to dissolve. In a stand mixer fitted with the dough hook attachment, add the flours, salt water, and olive oil. Turn the mixer to low and mix until combined, then increase the speed to medium and continue mixing until the dough comes together in a smooth ball, pulls away from the sides of the bowl, and is no longer sticky, 10 to 15 minutes. Wrap the dough tightly in plastic wrap and refrigerate for at least 1 hour (or up to overnight).

Line a baking sheet with parchment paper and sprinkle with semolina flour. Remove the dough from the refrigerator and slice off a 1-inch strip, then slice that in half. Roll both pieces into ropes about ½ inch thick, then cut the ropes crosswise into ½-inch-thick pieces.

To shape the cavateddi, hold a fork in your non-dominant hand with the tines pointing down. Use your thumb to press into the center of a piece of dough, pushing it against the back of the fork. Apply gentle pressure, pushing away from you, and roll the piece of dough off the fork. The dough will curve around your thumb, the two edges rising above the depressed center, and ridges will have formed on the back. With a bench scraper or knife, transfer the cavateddi to the prepared baking sheet, arranging them so they don't touch. Continue until all of the dough is used. Let the pasta dry slightly at room temperature, uncovered, for 30 to 45 minutes. Cook right away or wrap the baking sheet tightly with plastic wrap and refrigerate; the formed, uncooked pasta will keep overnight.

Bring a large pot of water to a boil and salt it generously. Add the pasta (in batches if necessary), return the water to a boil, and boil until pasta pieces float to the surface and remain there for 1 to 2 minutes. Taste a piece; it should be tender but chewy. If serving with a ragu, use a slotted spoon to transfer the cavateddi to a saucepan over low heat. Add the ragu and a small amount of pasta-cooking water and cook, tossing, until the cavateddi is well coated with glossy sauce, adding more pasta-cooking water as necessary. The cavateddi can also be boiled and served simply, tossed with butter and grated Parmigiano-Reggiano cheese.

PASTA, RAGU, RISOTTO & EGGS

BEEF & PORK RAGU

MAKES 6 CUPS

I keep a jar of this ragu in my fridge all the time—it's a convenient staple that gets better with age and can be used as a sauce for pasta or to top polenta, spoon onto fried eggs, or enrich cooked vegetables. This is a great way to highlight the flavor of grass-fed, free-range beef. The long, slow cooking will liquify any connective tissue, giving the ragu a supple texture. For an especially flavorful sauce, ask your butcher to grind beef and pork shank meat for you—the density of connective tissues in those cuts translates into rich, deep flavor. This sauce freezes beautifully, and the recipe can be doubled.

2 tablespoons extra-virgin olive oil

1 pound ground beef

1 pound ground pork

1 cup sofritto (page 17)

1 cup Bone Broth (page 20) or Roasted Bird Broth (page 18)

4 cups homemade tomato passato (page 24) or store-bought tomato puree

2 bay leaves

Kosher salt and freshly ground black pepper

In a large, high-sided Dutch oven or heavy pot, heat the olive oil over medium-high heat. When the oil is hot, add about ½ pound of the ground meat. Cook, stirring and breaking up large chunks with a wooden spoon, until the meat is beginning to brown. Add another ½ pound of the meat and continue the process until all of the meat has been added. When the last batch of meat is no longer pink, use a slotted spoon to transfer all of the meat to a bowl.

Add the sofritto to the now-empty pot and fry for 1 minute, then pour in the broth and use the wooden spoon to scrape up any browned bits sticking to the bottom of the pan. Return the meat to the pan and add the tomato puree and bay leaves. Season with a few teaspoons of salt and a teaspoon of pepper. Bring to a boil, then lower the heat so the liquid is barely simmering, and cook, stirring occasionally, until the sauce is thick and the meat is very soft, about 4 hours. Season to taste with additional salt and pepper.

The sauce can be eaten the same day it's made or cooled and refrigerated for a week. For longer storage, transfer the cooled ragu to plastic storage bags and place in the freezer. Frozen, it will keep for up to 6 months.

TAJARIN WITH SAGE & BUTTER

MAKES ABOUT 1 POUND; SERVES 4 TO 6

Tajarin is the Piedmontese dialect's name for tagliarini, a thin, flat noodle. It's very rich and has a deep yellow color, owing to the large quantity of egg yolks in the pasta dough. Typically, *tajarin* is served with butter and sage or ragu. I love the simplicity of this pasta and the elegant look of a little nest of the cooked noodles dressed with butter and a few fried sage leaves.

3½ cups "OO" flour, plus more for dusting

2 teaspoons kosher salt

12 egg yolks

12 tablespoons (1½ sticks) unsalted butter

1 bunch fresh sage

Parmigiano-Reggiano cheese, for serving (optional, this is not traditional but I like it)

In a stand mixer fitted with the dough hook attachment, combine the flour, salt, and egg yolks. Mix on low speed until combined, then increase the speed to medium and continue mixing the dough until it comes together in a smooth, supple ball, about 10 minutes. Drape the ball of dough in plastic wrap and let rest for 20 minutes. The dough can also be tightly wrapped in plastic and refrigerated overnight.

Cut the ball of dough into four equal pieces. Working with one ball at a time (keeping the other pieces covered with a clean kitchen towel or sheet of plastic wrap to prevent them from drying out), roll it with a rolling pin so it will fit through the widest setting of an electric or hand cranked pasta machine. Pass it through the widest setting of the pasta machine twice, then pass it through each subsequent setting until the dough is ⅛ to 1/16 inch thick. If you are rolling the dough by hand, roll each ball into a

4-inch disk with a rolling pin. Let the disks rest a few minutes (which lets the dough relax, making it easier to roll it thin) and roll again to double its diameter. Let rest again and roll a third time until you get the dough down to ⅛ to 1/16 inch thick.

If you are using a pasta machine, run the strips of dough through the finest grade cutter—the one that makes the smallest width noodles. If your pasta machine does not have cutters or if you are making entirely by hand, cut the dough into 7-inch lengths and roll each into a cylinder. With a sharp knife, cut cleanly through the rolled dough crosswise at ⅛-inch intervals into thin, delicate noodles.

Shake the cut noodles, dust liberally with flour, and set on a floured tray or towel. Repeat with the remaining dough. The cut noodles will keep for several hours at room temperature, draped with plastic wrap to prevent them from drying out.

Bring a large pot of salted water to a boil over high heat. While the water heats, melt the butter in a large frying pan over low heat. When the butter has melted, add the sage and keep warm over low heat (do not let the butter brown). When the water is boiling, cook the *tajarin* in batches until just tender, about 1 minute, letting the water return to a boil between batches. Using a spider or slotted spoon, transfer each batch of cooked *tajarin* to the warm butter. When all the *tajarin* has been cooked, add ½ cup of the pasta-cooking water to the pan with the *tajarin*, increase the heat to medium-low, and toss until the pasta is coated in butter. Divide the pasta among warmed plates and serve immediately with grated Parmigiano-Reggiano alongside.

BIRD & BUNNY RAGU

MAKES ABOUT 10 CUPS

I made this for the first time after an event at the Belcampo farm left me with a mixed bag of birds and bunnies. This lighter style of ragu—made by braising whole pieces of rabbit and guinea hen in a vinegar-spiked tomato sauce until exceptionally tender—is typical of the northern coast of Italy and is a favorite of mine in the spring and summer. I like to serve it over wide ribbons of fresh pasta, like tagliatelle or maltagliati (page 122), or spooned over cooked farro, barley, or polenta, finished with fresh thyme or shredded sage leaves, some cracked pepper, and grated Parmigiano-Reggiano cheese. This recipe makes a lot of ragu, but it freezes beautifully.

½ cup extra-virgin olive oil, or more as needed

1 rabbit (about 3 pounds), cut into 6 pieces

1 guinea hen or small (2½- to 3-pound) chicken, cut into 8 pieces

⅓ cup sofritto (page 17)

2 tablespoons all-purpose flour

1 tablespoon dried thyme

1 (750 ml) bottle dry white wine

1 (28-ounce) can whole peeled tomatoes

½ cup red wine vinegar

1 tablespoon kosher salt

1 (3 by 1-inch) Parmigiano-Reggiano rind

Cooked pasta, farro, barley, or polenta, for serving

Grated Parmigiano-Reggiano cheese, for serving

Preheat the oven to 200°F. Pour the olive oil into a large Dutch oven over medium-high heat. When the oil is hot but not smoking, add the rabbit and cook, turning once, until golden brown on both sides, about 6 minutes (depending on the size of your pan, you may need to do this in batches). Transfer to a rimmed plate. Repeat the process with the guinea hen, adding more olive oil to the pan as necessary.

When all of the meat has been seared, lower the heat to medium and add the sofritto to the pan. Cook, stirring, for 5 minutes, then add the flour and thyme and continue to cook, stirring, for 3 to 4 minutes. Pour in the wine and let cook for 5 minutes, using a wooden spoon to scrape off any browned bits sticking to the bottom of the pan. Pass the tomatoes through the widest plate of a food mill, or squeeze with your hands to break up, and add to the pot along with the vinegar, salt, and rind. Return the meat and any accumulated juices to the pot.

Cover the pot and transfer to the oven. Cook for 2 hours, until the meat is very tender and the sauce has reduced slightly. Remove the meat from the sauce and, when cool enough to handle, pull the meat from the bones and shred it into bite-size pieces. Discard the bones. Return the sauce to the stove top and reduce over medium heat until it has the consistency of ketchup, about 15 minutes.

Remove the rind and stir in the shredded meat. Increase the heat so the sauce is simmering vigorously and simmer for 5 minutes, until the meat is heated through. Serve over pasta, cooked farro or barley, or polenta, accompanied by grated Parmigiano-Reggiano cheese.

SQUASH & FARRO RISOTTO

SERVES 6

Farro risotto is fairly common at the trattorias that I used to frequent in northern Italy. It is a little easier to nail than a traditional risotto—the farro has a slightly longer window in which it remains al dente compared to rice. But, because farro is similarly starchy, it still becomes quite creamy when cooked slowly in liquid. Farro is hearty and nutty, and I think it pairs best with fall and winter vegetables, though there's no reason you couldn't make this year-round, substituting other vegetables for the squash and different herbs in place of the sage.

4 cups Bone Broth (page 20) or Roasted Bird Broth (page 18)

4 cups water

6 tablespoons unsalted butter

¼ cup Sofritto (page 17)

2 cups semipearled (semiperlato) farro

1 medium butternut squash, peeled and cut into 1-inch pieces (about 3 cups cubed squash)

2 tablespoons fresh sage

1 cup grated Parmigiano-Reggiano cheese

Pour the broth and water into a medium saucepan over medium heat and bring to a simmer.

In a large, high-sided pot over medium heat, melt 3 tablespoons of the butter. Add the sofritto and farro and cook, stirring, for 5 minutes.

Add the squash and sage and cook for 2 minutes more, then ladle in 1 cup of the hot broth. Lower the heat to medium-low and cook, stirring, for about 5 minutes, until all of the liquid has been absorbed. Ladle in another cup of broth.

Continue cooking, stirring constantly and adding broth as needed, until you have used all of the broth and the farro and squash are tender, 30 to 40 minutes. Remove from the heat and stir in the remaining 3 tablespoons butter and the Parmigiano-Reggiano. Transfer to a serving dish and serve hot.

FRESH TOMATO RISOTTO

SERVES 6

Though risotto is often considered a winter dish, this is one for summer, when you have a surplus of excellent tomatoes. Fresh tomato puree stands in for half of the broth, resulting in a lighter-bodied risotto packed with tomato flavor. Serve it as a stand-alone main course or as a side dish for grilled sausages or chicken. Any leftover risotto can be made into fritters: Let it come to room temperature, form it into balls, roll the balls in beaten egg, then bread crumbs, and deep-fry until golden for an indulgent little antipasto.

---

8 to 10 ripe medium tomatoes

1 quart Bone Broth (page 20) or Roasted Bird Broth (page 18)

2 tablespoons unsalted butter

2 cups Arborio rice

¼ cup sofritto (page 17)

1 cup grated Parmigiano-Reggiano cheese, plus more for serving

1 cup Crescenza cheese (if Crescenza is not readily available, substitute ½ cup mascarpone cheese)

Kosher salt

Torn basil, for garnish (optional)

Grate the tomatoes on the large holes of a box grater into a bowl, discarding the skins and any tough cores. Combine the tomato juice and pulp with the broth; you should have 8 cups of liquid. Transfer to a saucepan and warm over medium heat.

In a large heavy pan over medium-low heat, melt the butter. When the butter has melted, add the rice and cook, stirring, for 2 to 3 minutes, until the grains of rice begin to turn translucent. Add the sofritto and stir to combine. Add some of the tomato-broth mixture to the rice by the ladleful, stirring often and allowing each addition of liquid to be fully absorbed by the rice before adding more. Monitor the heat; the risotto should be bubbling faintly.

Continue adding liquid by the ladleful until it has all been incorporated and the rice is tender and creamy, about 30 minutes. Stir in the Parmigiano-Reggiano and Crescenza, season to taste with salt, and spoon into warmed bowls. Garnish with basil and serve immediately, accompanied by more grated Parmigiano-Reggiano.

VEGETABLES

STUFFED ZUCCHINI BLOSSOMS IN TOMATO SAUCE

SERVES 4

Most often, when you see zucchini blossoms on restaurant menus, they are stuffed with cheese, then battered and deep-fried. A deep-fried blossom is not a terrible thing, of course, but this recipe, where the flowers are stuffed with an herb-flecked ricotta cheese and braised in fresh tomato puree, is a lighter approach. One note: Do not overstuff the blossoms with the cheese mixture, or it will leak out when you pan-fry them.

1 cup whole-milk ricotta, store-bought or homemade (page 52)

½ cup finely grated Pecorino Romano

1 egg

¾ teaspoon kosher salt

1 bunch fresh basil, finely chopped

16 large zucchini blossoms

2 tablespoons extra-virgin olive oil

¼ cup sofritto (page 17)

3 cups homemade tomato passato, (page 24) or store-bought tomato puree

Crusty bread, pasta, or polenta, for serving

In a medium bowl, mix together the ricotta, Pecorino Romano, egg, ¼ teaspoon of the salt, and the basil.

Carefully open each zucchini blossom by making a slit on one side, taking care not to slice all the way through, checking for any bugs or dirt hidden within, and fill with about 2 teaspoons of the ricotta mixture, gently twisting the blossom closed.

Heat the olive oil in a large cast-iron pan over medium-high heat. When the oil is shimmering, add the stuffed blossoms in a single layer and cook, turning once, until lightly browned on both sides, about 2 minutes each side. Use a slotted spoon to gently transfer the blossoms to a plate.

Lower the heat to medium and add the sofritto. Cook, stirring, for 1 minute, then pour in the tomato puree. Stir in the remaining ½ teaspoon salt. Turn the heat down to low, cover, and let the tomato mixture reduce until thickened, about 20 minutes. Season to taste with additional salt.

Arrange the blossoms in a single layer on top of the tomato puree. Cover and cook for 10 minutes more, until the blossoms are heated through and the sauce is as thick as marinara sauce. Serve warm, accompanied by crusty bread or alongside pasta or polenta.

ZUCCHINI CARPIONE

SERVES 4 TO 6

In Italian, this preparation, where an ingredient is first fried and then packed in vinegar, is known as *carpione*. It was originally invented as a way to add flavor to carp fish from Lake Como, but now it's a preparation that's typically applied to vegetables. I was often served this in Piedmont, where the *carpione* originated and is still popular. Many homes would have a big glass terrine layered with all sorts of fried vegetables packed in vinegary brine, occasionally adding breaded, fried steaks to the mix . . . surprise! I usually make this with zucchini, though you can also substitute a medium butternut squash (pictured here) in fall, peeled, seeded, and cut as described below. Both pair well with dishes that can stand up to a healthy dose of acid, like the Fennel & Black Pepper–Crusted Pork Loin on page 219.

1½ cups water	6 medium zucchini, cut lengthwise into ¼-inch-thick slices, each slice cut in half crosswise
1 cup red wine vinegar	
2 teaspoons sugar	
1 teaspoon kosher salt	10 fresh sage leaves
Olive oil, for frying	Freshly ground black pepper

In a medium saucepan, combine the water, vinegar, sugar, and salt. Bring to a boil over high heat, then remove from the heat and let cool while you fry the zucchini.

Heat a 1-inch depth of olive oil in a large, high-sided pan over medium-high heat until hot but not smoking (it should register 325°F on a deep-frying thermometer). Fry the zucchini slices in batches, taking care to avoid overcrowding, until golden brown, about 3 minutes. Remove from the oil with a spider or slotted spoon and transfer to

a ceramic or glass terrine (do not use a metal pan, as the vinegar can react with the metal), layering the slices as necessary. Let the oil return to 325°F between batches.

Top the zucchini with the sage leaves and a few grinds of pepper, then pour the warm brine over. Transfer to the refrigerator and let rest overnight before eating; it will keep, refrigerated, for up to 1 week.

ROMANO BEAN SALAD

SERVES 4 TO 6

Fresh Romano beans are like the chubby cousin of green beans. You can slow-cook them with a bit of water and sofritto until silky and soft, one of my favorite ways to prepare them (though they end up looking murky camo green that way). Or you can make this salad where the beans remain brilliant green and have a crisp-tender texture. It's a natural side dish for grilled meat, or it can be topped with a soft-boiled egg for a very simple supper. It's best to dress the blanched beans right before you plan to serve them, as the lemon juice will cause the beans to discolor if they sit too long in the dressing.

Kosher salt

1 pound Romano beans, trimmed and cut into thirds

½ cup extra-virgin olive oil

¼ cup freshly squeezed lemon juice

1 cup chopped soft fresh herbs, such as parsley, chervil, chives, or mint

Flaky salt, such as Maldon

Freshly ground black pepper

Bring a pot of water to a boil and add salt. Add the beans and cook until just tender, about 3 minutes. Drain and let cool until warm, then transfer to a bowl and toss with olive oil, lemon juice, and herbs. Season to taste with flaky salt and pepper. Serve at room temperature.

BLISTERED GREEN BEANS

SERVES 6

This is an easy way to cook green beans that makes their flavor more complex, with deeply caramelized bits, a nice alternative to the traditional blanched bean. Great as a side dish, they're also terrific recycled into a salad the next day. If you'd like, these beans can be garnished with chopped fresh soft herbs, such as parsley, chervil, tarragon, or basil.

2 pounds green beans	Flaky salt, such as Maldon
2 tablespoons extra-virgin olive oil	Freshly ground black pepper
	1 lemon

Preheat the oven to 450°F. Top and tail the green beans and place in medium bowl. Add the olive oil, a healthy pinch of flaky salt, and a few grinds of black pepper.

Transfer the beans to a cast-iron skillet and spread them out into a single layer; if they are piled up, they will not roast well. Transfer to the oven and cook, stirring once, until the beans are softened and charred in spots, 12 to 15 minutes. Remove from the oven and squeeze lemon juice over to taste. Season to taste with additional salt and pepper. Serve warm or at room temperature.

LEMONY FENNEL SALAD

SERVES 4 TO 6

This is a great late fall or winter salad: it's elegant and simple and is a perfect complement to a rich main course. I like to let this salad chill out for at least 30 minutes before serving—a technique I use for any salad with fennel or kale in it—allowing the raw fennel to soften and the flavors to meld.

2 tablespoons salted capers

3 fennel bulbs, trimmed

2 teaspoons kosher salt

Juice of 1 lemon

2 tablespoons extra-virgin olive oil

2 tablespoons fresh parsley, finely chopped

Freshly ground black pepper

Soak the capers in warm water to cover for 15 minutes. Drain and rinse well. With a mandoline or very sharp knife, cut the fennel crosswise into paper-thin slices. Transfer to a bowl and season with salt, tossing to coat. Let stand for 5 minutes, then pour off any accumulated liquid. Add the lemon juice, olive oil, parsley, and capers and toss to combine. Season with freshly ground pepper and additional salt to taste. Let stand at room temperature for 30 minutes before serving.

SHAVED ZUCCHINI & CHEESE SALAD

SERVES 6

This is a recipe I stole from the opening chef at Belcampo's San Francisco restaurant. I first tasted it a few weeks before the restaurant opened in 2014 and immediately began making a version of it at home. You must use a mandoline to get really fine slices of zucchini (or have much better knife skills than I); sliced thin, the zucchini is spared that slightly mushy quality that mars most zucchini recipes. Though you can prepare the salad in advance, it should not be dressed until about 15 minutes before you plan to serve it, because it gets soggy if it sits any longer.

---

8 small zucchini

½ bunch (about 1½ cups) fresh Italian parsley leaves, roughly chopped

½ cup crumbled Toma cheese (see page 55) or queso fresco

¼ cup red wine vinegar

¼ cup extra-virgin olive oil

Kosher salt and freshly ground black pepper

Red pepper flakes

Using a mandoline, slice the zucchini into paper-thin rounds. Transfer to a bowl and add the parsley and cheese.

In a small bowl, whisk together the vinegar and olive oil. Pour the dressing over the zucchini and toss gently to combine. Let stand for 15 minutes, then season to taste with salt, freshly ground pepper, and red pepper flakes. Serve at room temperature.

GREEN TOMATO & CAPER SALAD

SERVES 4

In Sicily, green tomatoes are considered preferable to red for salads, and I developed a taste for their fresh, bright, acidic flavor when I lived there. This salad works best when made with very green, firm (unripe) tomatoes. If they are starting to ripen, the salad will become mushy rather than crisp. If you have a peppery, grassy olive oil—like *olio nuovo*—use it here. Serve this alongside rich grilled or confit meats.

---

2 tablespoons salted capers

4 large green (unripe) tomatoes

2 teaspoons kosher salt

1 cup fresh parsley leaves

¼ cup extra-virgin olive oil

Freshly ground black pepper

Freshly squeezed lemon juice (optional)

Soak the capers in warm water to cover for 15 minutes. Drain and rinse well. Core and slice the tomatoes into ¼-inch-thick slices using a mandoline or sharp knife. Put the sliced tomatoes in a bowl, add salt, and stir to combine. Let stand for 5 minutes, then drain off any liquid that has accumulated in the bowl.

Add the parsley leaves, soaked capers, and olive oil and mix well to combine. Season to taste with additional salt and pepper. Depending on the acidity of the tomatoes, you may want to add lemon juice to taste.

ARTICHOKES WITH LEMON & MINT

SERVES 4 TO 6

My early experiences with artichokes mostly involved using them as vehicles for funneling melted butter or hollandaise sauce into my mouth.

It wasn't until I moved to Sicily that I started to appreciate the choke. There, farmers sold them directly out of the trunks of cars parked by the side of the road. The choke came with the 3-foot-long stem attached (the stem, I learned, is also delicious), and I got used to bleeding fingertips after handling them, as each leaf of a Sicilian artichoke is topped with a long thorn.

Early in the season in Sicily, artichokes are eaten raw, finely sliced and left to soften in lemon juice. Later, as the buds toughen and mature, they are roasted whole on coals, fried straight with no batter, or stuffed and baked. The Italian phrase *la politica del carciofo* ("artichoke politics") refers to the strategy of dealing with your foes one at a time. The mature buds must be peeled slowly, the petals must be dealt with one by one—a little depressing when considered in the light of Sicilian politics.

This recipe for braised artichokes is also from my time in Sicily. It concentrates the flavors of the artichoke, which is especially useful given how much milder the American varietals are compared to their Italian counterparts.

Working with one artichoke at a time, break off the outer leaves until only pale green ones remain. Cut ½ inch off the top, trim the dark green parts around the stem, and peel the stem. Put the artichokes stem side up in a medium saucepan; they should be very tightly packed together.

Drizzle the artichokes with olive oil, then add enough water to the pan to reach the base of the artichokes. Season with salt, and tuck lemon slices between the artichokes and mint leaves.

Bring the water to a boil over high heat, then reduce the heat to low, cover, and cook until the artichokes are tender when pierced with the tip of a sharp knife, about 30 minutes. Remove the artichokes from the pot with a slotted spoon, transfer to a serving platter, and drizzle with more olive oil. Sprinkle with flaky salt. Serve warm or at room temperature.

10 artichokes

Extra-virgin olive oil, for drizzling

1 teaspoon kosher salt

1 lemon, thinly sliced

½ cup fresh mint leaves

Flaky salt, such as Maldon, for serving

BLOOD ORANGE SALAD

SERVES 4

In late fall and winter, this salad is an antidote to the limited selection of fresh vegetables at the farmers' market or grocery store. I like to make it with blood oranges, which are a little tart, but you can use pretty pink Cara Cara oranges, navels or, for an especially attractive salad, a mixture of all three.

4 blood oranges

1 fennel bulb, trimmed and thinly sliced

½ small red onion or 5 green onions (both white and green parts), thinly sliced

½ teaspoon kosher salt

¼ cup piquant extra-virgin olive oil, like olio nuovo

2 tablespoons fresh parsley, chopped

Pinch of red pepper flakes

Flaky sea salt, such as Maldon, for serving

With a sharp knife, cut off the top and bottom off each orange and stand them on a cutting board. Beginning at the top of each orange, cut down along the curve of the fruit to remove the skin and pith, then cut each orange crosswise into ¼-inch-thick slices. Transfer to a bowl and add the sliced fennel, onion, and kosher salt and mix gently but thoroughly to combine.

Transfer to a platter and drizzle with the olive oil, then top with the parsley and red pepper flakes. Season with flaky sea salt and serve.

BITTER GREENS WITH BUTTERMILK DRESSING

SERVES 4

It's easy to make pretty much any rough winter greens into salad with this dressing—the natural acidity in the buttermilk, combined with salt and lemon, softens and tenderizes even the toughest brassicas if given enough time. Once the greens have softened, drain off the excess liquid and dress with your best olive oil. I often top this with a sprinkling of nutritional yeast to add some umami—if you like nutritional yeast for its flavor or health benefits, give it a try.

---

4 bunches bitter greens, such as mustard greens, kale, or dandelion greens (or a mixture), washed and stemmed

1 cup buttermilk (page 23)

1 tablespoon freshly squeezed lemon juice

1 tablespoon kosher salt

2 tablespoons extra-virgin olive oil

1 ounce shaved Parmigiano-Reggiano cheese shaved with a vegetable peeler (optional)

Nutritional yeast (optional)

Finely chop the greens and transfer to a large bowl. Whisk together the buttermilk, lemon juice, and salt, pour over the greens, and toss to coat. Let stand at room temperature for 30 minutes. Drain any excess liquid from the bowl, drizzle with olive oil, add the Parmigiano-Reggiano cheese, and toss again. Season to taste with additional salt and nutritional yeast.

EGGPLANT CAPONATA

SERVES 4 TO 6

Caponata is both a sweet-savory side salad and a condiment that exalts the sweet ripeness of summer. Therefore, it should really be made only when you have access to great eggplants and tomatoes. If you're able to make the caponata a day before you want to serve it, you'll be rewarded for your forethought, as it only gets better with time. Caponata is excellent served alongside grilled meats, as a stand-alone side dish, as a condiment for a sandwich or sausage, paired with ricotta as a topping for garlicky toasts, or tossed with pasta.

Olive oil, for frying

6 medium eggplants, cut into 1-inch cubes (about 12 cups cubed eggplant)

1 large yellow onion, diced

3 cups diced tomatoes

1 cup sliced hearts of celery plus 2 tablespoons chopped celery leaves

½ cup red wine vinegar

½ cup capers

5 anchovy fillets, finely chopped

1 tablespoon sugar

Kosher salt and freshly ground black pepper

½ cup pine nuts, toasted, for garnish

Heat a 1-inch depth of olive oil in a heavy, high-sided frying pan over medium-high heat. Working in batches, fry the cubed eggplant until golden brown, about 3 minutes per batch. Remove the cooked eggplant with a slotted spoon and let drain on paper towels.

When all of the eggplant has been fried, pour off all but ½ cup of the olive oil from the pan and lower the heat to medium. Add the onion and cook, stirring often, until light golden brown, about 5 minutes. Turn the heat down to medium-low and add the tomatoes, celery hearts, vinegar, capers, anchovies, and sugar and simmer, stirring occasionally, for 15 minutes. Stir in the fried eggplant and continue simmering for 30 minutes more, until most of the liquid has cooked off and the mixture is thick. Season to taste with salt and pepper.

Transfer to a serving bowl and let cool. Garnish with the celery leaves and pine nuts and serve warm or at room temperature.

EASY SEARED MUSHROOMS

SERVES 4

This is a very quick and easy side dish for fall and winter, something I often make and serve alongside steak. I like to use a mixture of mushrooms for textural contrast.

---

2 tablespoons extra-virgin olive oil

4 cups mushrooms, such as cremini, oyster, or shiitake

1 sprig fresh thyme

1 teaspoon kosher salt

1 cup Roasted Bird Broth (page 18)

2 tablespoons unsalted butter

Heat a medium cast-iron frying pan over high heat and add the oil. When the oil is hot, add the mushrooms and thyme to the pan. The mushrooms will immediately begin to leach out water; cook, stirring, until there is no longer liquid in the pan and the mushrooms are beginning to brown.

Lower the heat to medium-high, season the mushrooms with salt, then add the broth, cover, and cook for 2 minutes. Uncover and cook until there is no more liquid in the pan, about 3 minutes. Stir in the butter, then season to taste with additional salt. Serve warm.

TORTA DI VERDURE

MAKES ONE 10-INCH PIE; SERVES 6 TO 8

I love this dish, a rich savory pie made with whatever greens I find at the farmers' market. I've made it with kale, Swiss chard, collard greens, radish tops, beet greens, half a bunch of parsley—if it's green and leafy, it's going in the torta! A generous amount of olive oil and grated Parmigiano-Reggiano enriches the greens and prevents the torta from feeling too restrained, too healthful. Serve thin wedges of this as a starter.

FOR THE DOUGH

2 cups all-purpose flour

1 cup water

2 tablespoons extra-virgin olive oil

1 teaspoon kosher salt

FOR THE FILLING

4 bunches kale, Swiss chard, beet greens, collard greens, radish greens, or a mixture, thick center ribs removed and discarded, leaves torn into large pieces (about 16 cups raw greens)

2 eggs

2 cups grated Parmigiano-Reggiano, aged Asiago, or dry Jack cheese

1 cup extra-virgin olive oil, plus more for brushing

1 tablespoon kosher salt, plus more for sprinkling

½ teaspoon grated nutmeg

Make the dough: In a stand mixer fitted with the dough hook attachment, combine the flour, water, olive oil, and salt. Mix on medium speed until a smooth dough forms, then wrap the dough ball in plastic and let rest at room temperature while you make the filling.

CONTINUED

Make the filling: Wash the greens well. In a large pot, bring a few inches of water to a boil. When the water is boiling, add the greens and cook until they wilt, about 2 minutes. (Depending on the size of your pot, you may need to do this in batches.) Transfer the wilted greens to a colander and let cool. When cool enough to handle, grab handfuls and squeeze firmly over the sink to remove as much liquid as possible. Transfer to the bowl of a food processor.

Add the eggs, cheese, olive oil, salt, and nutmeg to the food processor and pulse until the greens are finely chopped and the mixture is well combined.

Preheat the oven to 375°F. Transfer the dough to a floured work surface and cut into two pieces, one slightly larger than the other. With a rolling pin, roll the larger piece of dough into a circle about 12 inches in diameter and transfer to a 10-inch round cast-iron frying pan or ceramic pie plate, leaving the overhang. Add the filling, smoothing it into an even layer. Roll the second piece of dough into a 10-inch circle and use it to top the pie. Pull the overhanging dough over the top piece of dough to seal, then cut a few steam vents in the top crust with the tip of a sharp knife or a pair of scissors.

Brush the top of the pie with olive oil, sprinkle with salt, and bake until golden brown, about 1 hour. Remove from the oven, let cool slightly, then cut into wedges. Serve warm.

FAST KRAUT

SERVES 4

This is one of my go-to recipes for a quick vegetable side, especially handy as cabbages can last a long time in your refrigerator. Cooking cabbage brings out its natural sweetness, balanced here by a lashing of cider vinegar. I especially like this dish paired with sausages, duck confit, or fatty roasts.

---

1 green or red cabbage (about 2 pounds)

1 cup warm water

2 tablespoons cider vinegar

2 teaspoons kosher salt

1 tablespoon duck fat or unsalted butter

1 teaspoon fennel seeds

Freshly ground black pepper

Peel any ugly outer leaves from the cabbage and discard, core, and chop into 1-inch-thick ribbons.

In a measuring cup stir together the water, vinegar, and salt, stirring to dissolve the salt.

In a large cast-iron frying pan over high heat, melt the duck fat. When the fat is hot, add the cabbage and sear without stirring for 3 minutes (this will give the cabbage time to develop some tasty crispy brown bits). Add the water mixture and cook stirring occasionally until the cabbage is wilted and tender, 5 to 7 minutes, and the water has evaporated. Stir in the fennel seeds and season to taste with additional salt and freshly ground black pepper. Serve warm or at room temperature.

BLACKENED CARROTS

SERVES 4

I often end up with a miserable bag of carrots at the bottom of my refrigerator, and this recipe is how I deal with them. (I can't be the only person with this problem, right?) Peeled and roasted whole, even slightly droopy carrots turn into a great side dish, equally good fresh from the oven or as leftovers. Roasting the carrots in lard adds some rich, meaty flavor to this dish, a nice counterpoint to carrots' natural sweetness, but olive oil or butter works just as well. Embrace the burnt bits: some blackening on the carrots makes them taste great. Ideally, choose carrots that are no thicker than ¾ inch so you can roast them whole; if yours are much fatter, cut them down to size before roasting.

---

16 thin carrots, peeled and topped

2 tablespoons melted lard (page 21), olive oil, or unsalted butter

1½ teaspoons kosher salt

Preheat the oven to 450°F. In a cast-iron pan, toss the carrots with the lard to coat, then season with salt. Transfer to the oven and roast until blistered and tender, shaking the pan occasionally so the carrots brown on all sides, about 40 minutes. Serve hot or at room temperature.

SEARED RADICCHIO WITH BAGNA CAUDA

SERVES 4 TO 6

Garlic and anchovies melted in butter is a great accompaniment to the bitter, complex flavor of seared radicchio. If you do not have the time to make bagna cauda, you can cheat: simply melt some butter and toss a few minced anchovy fillets and a clove of thinly sliced garlic into it.

---

4 small heads radicchio, cut in half

½ cup Bagna Cauda (page 32)

Freshly squeezed lemon juice

Kosher salt and freshly ground black pepper

Heat a large, dry cast-iron frying pan or griddle over high heat until very hot. Lay the radicchio halves in the dry pan, cut side down, and cook until they are deeply browned on the cut side, about 5 minutes. Remove from the pan and cut each radicchio half into two pieces.

Transfer the radicchio quarters to a platter, drizzle with the bagna cauda, and use your hands to toss the radicchio in the bagna cauda so it's coated all over. Season to taste with lemon juice and salt and pepper and transfer to a platter; serve warm or at room temperature.

CORNMEAL SPOONBREAD

MAKES ONE 8-INCH SPOONBREAD; SERVES 6

Spoonbread, so named because it's soft enough to serve and eat with a spoon, is a traditional side dish in the American South. But the Italians love their cornmeal, too, so this recipe does not feel out of place in my largely rustic Italian recipe repertoire. Some recipes for spoonbread suggest separating the eggs, mixing the yolks into the cornmeal mixture, then beating the whites until stiff and folding them in. This gives you a slightly fluffier texture, but either way the spoonbread will deflate when you pull it from the oven, so I've never bothered with that extra step.

2 cups whole milk

1 cup stoneground medium-fine yellow cornmeal

6 tablespoons unsalted butter

1 teaspoon kosher salt

4 eggs, at room temperature

Preheat the oven to 375°F. In a medium saucepan over medium heat, bring the milk to just below the boil. Reduce the heat to low and whisk in the cornmeal. Cook over low heat, whisking constantly, for 3 minutes, then whisk in 4 tablespoons of the butter and the salt.

Remove the pan from the heat and whisk in the eggs. Melt the remaining 2 tablespoons butter in an 8-inch cast-iron frying pan over low heat. Swirl the pan so the butter coats the bottom and partway up the sides, then pour in the batter.

Bake for 40 minutes, until puffed, golden, and set. It will deflate when you remove it from the oven. Serve warm.

TROTTER BEANS

SERVES 6 TO 8

Dried beans are a favorite winter staple for me, particularly when cooked in trotter broth, which makes them especially rich and silky. It's astonishing the difference in both flavor and cooking between a dried bean that has been in long storage, sometimes for years, versus one that is freshly dried, harvested that season. I find that when I use dried beans that are of relatively recent vintage (no more than a year old), they cook evenly and well without being first soaked in water overnight. Rancho Gordo, in Napa, California, has a good variety of beans that are always from a recent harvest; they are available by mail order. Pinquitos, small pink beans that are often served alongside Santa Maria–style barbecue, are a favorite, but you can substitute another variety, such as cranberry, borlotti, or pinto.

This dish can be shaped by whatever leftovers you have in the fridge. Cooked greens are a great addition, as are small pieces of stewed meat or confit. I always toss in a few cubes of sofritto and a bit of either tomato sauce or tomato paste to give the dish some more complexity and acid. Serve the beans as a side dish, garnished with some fresh herbs and a ribbon of olive oil. Or, for a hearty main, serve the beans topped with cooked greens and a fried egg.

2 cups dried pinquito beans

1 cup Trotter Broth (page 18)

4 cups water

¼ cup Sofritto (page 17)

1 tablespoon tomato paste

2 dried bay leaves

Kosher salt

In a heavy pot combine the pinquito beans, broth, water, sofritto, tomato paste, and bay leaves. Bring to a boil over high heat, skimming any foam that rises to the surface, then lower the heat so the liquid is barely simmering.

Simmer gently, stirring occasionally, until the beans are tender, 3 to 4 hours, adding more liquid as necessary so that the beans look as if they're in a bathtub: neither completely swamped with liquid nor too dry. When the beans are approaching tenderness, season with salt. To determine doneness, taste five beans. If any of them is not tender, continue cooking until you get a five-bean sampling where all are. Serve warm, dressed up or down.

CHICKPEA TORTE

MAKES ONE 9-INCH TORTE; SERVES 6

This dish truly represents the beauty of *cucina povera*, the Italian gift of making something special with humble, inexpensive ingredients. In this torte, beans and eggs are dressed up with herbs and spices to make a meaty, rich, and satisfying meal. Italian cuisine is full of these tricks: a little butter, bread crumbs, and some cheese to make dishes a little richer, more savory, and toothsome without the addition of meat. This makes great leftovers, as it improves with age. Adding a pinch of baking soda to the soaking beans helps soften them (particularly if the beans are older) and reduces their carminative qualities.

---

2 cups dried chickpeas	2 teaspoons crushed red pepper flakes
Pinch of baking soda	1½ teaspoons kosher salt
½ cup plus 2 tablespoons extra-virgin olive oil	3 eggs
2 medium yellow onions, chopped	1 cup grated Parmigiano-Reggiano cheese
20 sage leaves	

Put the chickpeas and baking soda in a medium bowl and add cold water to cover. Let soak overnight.

The next day, drain and rinse the chickpeas and transfer to a heavy pot. Add water to cover by 1 inch, bring to a boil over high heat, then lower the heat so the liquid is simmering. Simmer until tender, 1 to 2 hours, then drain, reserving the cooking liquid, and set aside.

Meanwhile, in a large frying pan, heat ½ cup of the olive oil over medium heat. Add the onions and half of the sage and cook, stirring often, until the onions are very soft and golden brown, 25 to 30 minutes.

Preheat the oven to 375°F. Put the cooked onions and sage leaves in a food processor and add half of the cooked chickpeas. Process until almost smooth, adding a bit of the bean-cooking liquid as necessary to aid the blending. Transfer to a large bowl and add the remaining (whole) cooked chickpeas. Mince the remaining sage leaves and stir into the batter with the red pepper flakes and salt. Using your hands, squeeze the batter to crush the whole chickpeas slightly.

Stir in the eggs and Parmigiano-Reggiano cheese. Grease a 9-inch ovenproof frying pan or cake pan with the remaining 2 tablespoons olive oil. Spoon the chickpea batter into the pan, smoothing the top, and bake until browned on top and set, about 1 hour. Let cool on a wire rack, then cut into wedges and serve warm or at room temperature. Serve with a salad for a lunch or light dinner.

TALLOW FRIES

SERVES 4 TO 6

Homemade French fries are pretty awesome. And these, cooked in beef tallow until golden, are the ultimate version. Double frying ensures that the fries are creamy within with a crisp exterior and is worth the (nominal) extra effort. Serve these as a snack before a dinner party and watch your guests go crazy, or pair them with a grilled steak and a simple salad.

---

4 russet potatoes	Sea salt
8 cups Rendered Beef Fat (Tallow) (page 22), canola oil, or peanut oil	

Rinse the potatoes in water, then cut lengthwise into ½-inch-thick batons. Transfer to a bowl and cover with cold water. Let soak for at least 30 minutes or up to overnight (if soaking overnight, transfer the bowl to the refrigerator).

Preheat the oven to 300°F. Melt the tallow in a heavy, high-sided pot over medium-high heat.

While the oil heats, remove the potatoes from the water and dry very thoroughly with clean kitchen towels or paper towels. Line a baking sheet with paper towels and set nearby.

When the tallow reaches 370°F, carefully add some of the potatoes to the pot, taking care not to overcrowd. Fry the potatoes for 3 minutes, then transfer to the baking sheet with tongs or a spider. Fry the remaining potatoes in batches, letting the oil return to 370°F between batches.

When all of the potatoes have been fried, bring the tallow to 380°F. Working in batches, fry the potatoes a second time, until they are golden brown and crisp, 3 to 4 minutes more. Transfer back to the paper towel–lined baking sheet and keep warm in the oven until all the potatoes are cooked. Just before serving, season with sea salt. Eat hot.

ASADO POTATOES

SERVES 6

I first ate these crispy potatoes at a Uruguayan asado—a South American barbecue—where they were cooked in a Dutch oven alongside the grilling meats, and the method has become my favorite way to prepare russets. They are easy to make, and the result is fairly spectacular, giving you the best of both worlds—tender, buttery rounds of potato with browned, crunchy edges. Don't pack the sliced potatoes into the pan too tightly—tight enough to remain upright but with still a bit of space between the slices, so the heat can circulate and cook the potatoes through. They are equally delicious prepared with olive oil or melted duck fat instead of butter.

6 large russet potatoes

12 tablespoons (1½ sticks) unsalted butter, melted

Kosher salt and freshly ground black pepper

Preheat the oven to 450°F. Wash and scrub the potatoes and, with a mandoline or sharp knife, slice the potatoes into ⅛-inch-thick slices and put in a bowl. Toss with half of the butter, then arrange the potatoes in a spiral in a 10-inch cast-iron pan. Season with salt and pepper.

Roast the potatoes until tender and brown and crispy on top, about 45 minutes. Remove from the oven, pour the remaining butter over, and season to taste with additional salt and pepper. Serve hot.

Cooking in cast-iron

I first began cooking in cast-iron using a Dutch oven, one of those old-fashioned ones with little legs and a top with a deep edge around it for holding coals. I spent a summer in college teaching outdoor cookery to kids, and part of that experience was teaching myself how many glowing embers needed to be piled onto the lid to make campfire brownies that were neither burnt nor goopy on top—high stakes when you consider my audience. After I learned my way around that first Dutch oven, I became a real devotee of cast-iron pans, enamored of their versatility, relative indestructibility, and, often, storied past. I was endlessly ridiculed by my family for having once made a boyfriend lug a 20-inch cast-iron skillet with us on a backpacking trip (it was love!), and I had one or two small ones with me throughout my itinerant twenties living in Sicily and Piedmont.

Unlike other pans, cast-iron is truly an all-in-one cooking vessel. You can braise in it, fry in it, bake in it. A well-seasoned cast-iron pan has a coating of polymerized oil, which is remarkably tough and very difficult to destroy. Soap won't ruin the seasoning. A metal spoon or spatula won't destroy the seasoning. Stacking your cast-iron pans together won't cause the tough-as-nails seasoning to chip off. Even cooking something acidic in the pan won't degrade the coating or add a metallic taste to the dish (a popular myth). Not only are cast-iron pans remarkably resilient, but I also believe that they're better for the environment. The best among them are vintage, the ultimate in reuse, only improving with time if well maintained. And I suspect that were I to bury a cast-iron pan in a patch of dirt, it would biodegrade in the space of a decade. I don't know how many half-lives you'd need for a Teflon pan.

Buying cast-iron

Though you can purchase new cast-iron pans (both unseasoned and preseasoned),
I encourage you to seek out an old skillet or Dutch oven for your kitchen the next
time you are at a flea market or yard sale. Though both vintage and modern cast-iron
pans are still cast in sand molds, the vintage ones were subjected to an additional
polishing step that gave the pans an especially satiny finish. As production scaled up
in cast-iron factories following World War II, that polishing step was dropped, and
so modern cast-iron has a slightly rougher finish. For many applications (like a braise
or deep frying), this manufacturing change has no noticeable impact at all. For other
uses—like frying an egg or searing a steak—I find that the smoother, older cast-iron
just does a better job. The older cast-iron is also slightly lighter weight. I can flip an egg
single-handedly in one of my vintage frying pans but can't in a new one. It's not a big
difference, but it's noticeable when you rely on these pans a lot.

For a new pan with that vintage feel, seek out Japan-made cast-iron pans. In Japan, many
of the producers still include the final polishing step as part of the manufacturing
process, so even a new pan has that amazing finish that typically comes from years of
dedicated use and care. Unfortunately, it costs about ten times as much as American
cast-iron. Years ago, when I was a judge on *The Next Iron Chef*, shooting in Tokyo,
I headed over to the city's cookware district and dropped a ludicrous sum of money
on a modern cast-iron wok with a wooden lid. It felt crazy at the time, but now, after
five years of cooking in that pot at least twice a week, it seems like a (relatively) good
investment.

Caring for cast-iron

Cast-iron pans have a reputation for being hard to maintain because when they're
improperly cared for, they almost immediately develop a flush of red rust, which can
be worrisome. If you see a gently rusted pan at the flea market, all is not lost, provided
the rust is only surface deep. It requires only a scrubbing and reseasoning to restore it
to its former glory.

To clean a dirty cast-iron skillet, run hot water over it and use steel wool to remove any
crud. If it's not really greasy, try to stick just with hot water, but if it's really dirty, you

can use a little squirt of dish soap. To clean a *really* dirty cast-iron skillet, you can run it through the dishwasher, though I don't advise doing this too frequently, as it will eventually damage the patina that gives seasoned cast-iron its nonstick qualities.

Always dry your cast-iron immediately after washing by wiping it really dry with a towel or setting it on a lit burner until any liquid evaporates; never let it sit in a sink full of water. Once the cast-iron is dry, if the surface looks matte, rub a bit of cooking oil into the pan to maintain its seasoning. Properly cared for, a cast-iron pan can—and probably will—outlast you.

FISH & MEAT

SALMON CONFIT TWO WAYS

SERVES 6 TO 8

For anyone who's ever overcooked an expensive piece of fish (I am raising my hand here), take heart: this technique—of cooking salmon slowly in fat—is almost impossible to mess up and yields succulent, perfectly cooked salmon.

When I was a kid growing up in Eugene, Oregon, my dad would buy fresh, wild salmon out of a cooler at our local gas station for about a buck a pound (I am not making this up). At those prices, we ate salmon about twice a week, and my dad loved experimenting with new ways to cook it. For a while, he was obsessed with the faddish method of wrapping a fillet in a million layers of aluminum foil and cooking it in the dishwasher.

The two types of confit—one cooked in butter and the other jarred in olive oil—are equally luxurious and delicious, both beautiful ways of cooking fresh fish. The butter-poached salmon is best pulled from the butter while still warm, then broken into chunks and served over greens, cooked green beans, or boiled potatoes dressed with the salmon's cooking butter and a squeeze of lemon.

The olive oil confit is best eaten after it has sat overnight in the refrigerator. Let it come to room temperature, and it can be used in the same way that you might use a high-quality canned tuna: served with butter beans, in a salad with lemon and herbs, or mixed with capers and herbs and used as a sandwich filling. This preparation requires two quart-size mason jars or one half-gallon mason jar.

BUTTER-POACHED SALMON

1 (2-pound) fillet wild salmon, skin on

1 tablespoon kosher salt

2 pounds (8 sticks) salted butter, melted

1 dried bay leaf

Zest of 1 lemon, removed with a vegetable peeler

With a pair of tweezers, remove the pin bones from the salmon and season on both sides with salt. Refrigerate for at least 4 or up to 12 hours. Rinse the fish and pat dry with paper towels, then place skin side down in a heavy pot large enough to accommodate the fillet without bending it.

Pour the butter over (it should just cover the fish) and add the bay leaf and lemon zest. Cook over low heat until the fish is opaque, about 15 minutes. Let cool to room temperature in the butter. If eating right away, remove the fish from the butter, peel off and discard the skin, and break the fillet into large chunks. If storing, let stand in the butter until cool, then wrap tightly and refrigerate for up to 4 days. Before serving, gently reheat over low heat until the butter melts, then gently remove the fish.

CONTINUED

OLIVE OIL–POACHED SALMON

1½ pounds wild salmon, skinned

2 teaspoons kosher salt

1 Meyer lemon, quartered

10 sprigs Italian parsley

2 cloves garlic, crushed

Extra-virgin olive oil

With a pair of tweezers, remove the pin bones from the salmon and season on both sides with salt. Refrigerate for at least 4 or up to 12 hours. Rinse the fish and pat dry with paper towels, then cut crosswise into 2-inch-wide pieces.

Pack the fish chunks, lemon quarters, parsley, and garlic into two quart-sized (or one half-gallon) mason jars and top with olive oil to within 1 inch of the top rim. Seal the jars tightly, then transfer to a large pot. Add enough water to the pot to cover the jar by 1 inch. Bring the water to a boil, then remove from the heat and let the jar sit in the water until it has cooled to room temperature. Remove from the water and use immediately, or transfer to the refrigerator and refrigerate for up to 4 days. Bring to room temperature before serving.

CRACKED CRABS WITH LEMON-CHILE VINAIGRETTE

SERVES 6

My dear friend Angelo Garro taught me this recipe, which has become one of my favorite ways to prepare crab. It's an especially beloved preparation because it requires very little work, just making a robust vinaigrette to toss with a cooked cracked crab that you get from the fish counter.

Angelo grew up in Siracusa, Sicily, and we bonded over a shared love for the foods and language of the region. For several years, Angelo had a successful blacksmith business, while making charcuterie and all sorts of amazing food and feasts on the side. He recently made his sideline interest in food into his main business, Omnivore, which produces a flavored salt inspired by Angelo's Sicilian palate and roots.

What I like about this recipe is that it moves the crab in a very Mediterranean direction, different from the traditional Northern California method of serving it with lots of melted butter or aioli. Angelo often roasts whole crabs on the open fire and then tosses them with vinaigrette, which is a delicious thing to do if you feel like grilling and prefer warm crab. Otherwise, you can get whole cooked, cleaned, and cracked crabs.

This is a great dish to serve piled high on a big serving platter at the center of a newspaper-covered table—let people dig in and get in up to their elbows.

½ cup extra-virgin olive oil

½ cup freshly squeezed lemon juice

8 cloves garlic, smashed to a coarse paste

1 tablespoon red pepper flakes

Kosher salt

Cracked black pepper

2 cups fresh parsley leaves

6 Dungeness crabs, cooked, cleaned, and cracked; chilled

Crusty bread, for serving

In a medium bowl, whisk together the olive oil, lemon juice, garlic, and red pepper flakes. Season to taste with salt and pepper, then stir in the parsley leaves.

Put the crab in a large bowl and pour the vinaigrette over. Toss with your hands so all of the crab pieces are coated in vinaigrette. Transfer to a platter and let stand for 10 minutes before eating. Serve with crusty bread alongside for mopping up the surplus vinaigrette that collects on the platter.

How to make great food

My style of cooking evolved from years of being immersed in a variety of food cultures and making a career around an interest in old foodways and recipes. In retrospect, I have a few watershed moments of culinary growth that I can trace back to specific moments in my life. And these are the basic principles that have stuck with me, the lessons I learned over time that have made me a better cook.

Better ingredients

Now it's common knowledge that better ingredients translate to better food, but it was truly a revelation for me when I first started working in dairies and visiting farm kitchens in Europe. Most meals consisted of a bowl of good olives, a piece of fresh cheese, boiled eggs with orange yolks sprinkled with herbs and salt, and a bowl of really sweet little tomatoes followed by one simple rustic dish like a soup or a pasta. The food was far, far simpler than I'd had and also far, far more delicious.

At the time, I'd never considered that humble ingredients—things I'd typically used to make other, more complex dishes—could be stand-alone stars. I did not know, for example, that really good butter could be as delicious as any cheese, especially when you make it yourself (page 23). Upon returning to the States, I started to seek out better food. I'd shopped at farmers' markets and was accustomed to buying fresh fruits and vegetables in season. But I started to look at other parts of my grocery list and began purchasing farm-fresh eggs laid by free-ranging chickens, cheeses produced by small artisan farms, good creamery butter. I also began investing in either farm-verified olive oil from a California supplier or farm-sourced and organic-certified oil from European producers after learning that most of the so-called extra-virgin olive oil sold in the United States is actually not extra virgin and in fact not even 100 percent olive oil. Better ingredients allowed me to be, in general, a lazier cook and still take all the credit for a great meal. When you have amazing simple ingredients of the highest order, get out of the way and let them shine.

Sugar, salt, and acid

Sicily, where I spent a few years living and working in my twenties, is a land of extreme culinary contrasts. Very ripe sheep's milk ricotta with a barny, musky flavor is paired with lots of sugar and a bitter almond marzipan to make cassata cake, a traditional dessert. Fillets of salt-cured anchovies, briny and rich, are mixed with hot chiles and thinly sliced lemon for a fresh, bracing salad. Some of these dishes were born of practicality. The island is incredibly hot, and in the era before refrigeration, salt and sugar—both natural preservatives—were used to keep food safe. The Sicilian diet also includes an abundance of vinegar and citrus, raw alliums, and chiles, all traditionally used for the same reasons, to extend the shelf life of foods and to decrease the possibility of contamination. Though there's no longer a practical need for it, these ingredients are now the backbone of the regional diet. The islanders are famous for their *agrodolce* dishes, that are equally sweet, salty, and acidic. The typical dish of Sicily, caponata, showcases this combination. Every farm meal I ate with my friends and colleagues in Sicily had an element of *agrodolce*, sometimes surprisingly, like the time I bit into a ravioli dressed in salty pork *sugo* and discovered it was stuffed with super sweet ricotta. Some of those extreme pairings were too much contrast for my American palate. But the core lesson, that of balancing the sweetness, saltiness, and acidity in a recipe was not lost on me. I finally understood why restaurant food often tastes better than its homemade counterpart—chefs have this balance figured out: they add a pinch or two of sugar to savory sauces, salt more heavily, and balance that saltiness with acid, bringing everything into harmony. In my own cooking, I'm always striving for that balance, introducing acidic elements to my dishes in the form of vinegar or lemon juice, salting my food throughout the cooking process, rather than just at the very end, and constantly tasting the food as I go.

Don't freak out about your tools

I remember a dinner made by a farm wife in Sicily that blew my mind: fresh pasta with tomato sauce, and local cheese, accompanied by an orange and green onion salad (similar to the one on page 148). I went into the kitchen with her after we'd finished eating and looked around. Like many of the great Sicilian home chefs I got to know, she had only one knife and it wasn't particularly sharp. But what surprised me was the rest of the kit used to make the dinner: a wooden board, a fork, and a piece of sheet metal pierced with a nail to make a dozen holes that worked as an improvised cheese grater and/or tomato seeder. Because I grew up in a culture where margarita makers,

banana slicers, and other single-use objects exist, the idea of a kitchen outfitted with only a couple of tools was amazing to me. I try to make sure that any new piece of cooking equipment that I buy can do at least two things well. This helps distinguish things that I will use every day from the tool that will molder at the back of a cabinet. The point being, you do not need an extensive arsenal of tools in order to make good food. It's better to have fewer, better quality items, like one or two good sharp knives and a couple of cast-iron pans in different sizes—you'll be surprised by what you can make with just those tools.

Wood fire cooking

I had not fully explored wood fire cookery until my work with Belcampo took me frequently to South America. There I learned the beauty of a long afternoon noodling around with a wood fire, cooking food over coals. South American cooks taught me the importance of fully burning down wood to the embers, how to adjust the grill and move your meat and vegetables around to the different zones, each at a different temperature, much like moving a pan on the stove top from a hot burner to a cooler one. More than any type of cooking, I find wood fire cooking meditative in that it makes you slow down to its schedule and adapt to an ancient way of doing things (right up there with kneading bread, actually, in terms of in-kitchen meditative states). Learning to cook over live fire is probably one of the most traditional skills there is, and one that has given me so much pleasure.

SQUID & BEANS

SERVES 4

This recipe is inspired by a dish I love at Camino restaurant in Oakland, which is owned and operated by friends of mine, Russell Moore and Allison Hopelain. The food at Camino is primarily cooked over an open hearth, and the menu often features Russell's take on traditional dishes, like this classic pairing of squid and beans, lightened and refreshed with fresh shelling beans and a bright tomato puree. Russell cooks his version over an open fire; I do mine in a clay pot set on the stove top.

2 tablespoons extra-virgin olive oil, plus more for drizzling

½ cup Sofritto (page 17)

2 cups fresh shelling beans

3 cups homemade tomato passato (page 24) or store-bought tomato puree

Kosher salt

8 whole fresh squid, cleaned, separated into bodies and tentacles; bodies cut into rings

1 cup fresh parsley, coarsely chopped

In a medium pot over medium heat, heat 1 tablespoon of the olive oil. Add the sofritto and cook, stirring, for 1 minute. Add the beans and tomato puree and bring to a simmer; simmer until the beans are tender, stirring occasionally and tasting frequently for doneness, about 25 minutes. Season to taste with salt.

Heat the remaining tablespoon oil in a medium cast-iron frying pan over high heat. Season the squid with salt. When the pan is hot, add the squid and sear until the tentacles curl and the squid is opaque, 1 to 2 minutes. Add the cooked squid to the tomato and bean mixture and simmer for 5 minutes more, until the squid is tender. Season to taste with additional salt.

Transfer to a serving dish and stir in the parsley. To finish, drizzle with a ribbon of olive oil.

AGRODOLCE TONGUE

SERVES 4

I had my first experience with beef tongue when it was served to me as a cold lunchmeat during a childhood stint living in London. I had the startling, disconcerting realization while eating that it was actually, you know, the tongue of a cow, touching my own tongue. Heady stuff for a kid. Tongue has largely dropped out of our modern recipe repertory, which is a shame because the beauty of beef tongue is that it's extremely lean and absorbs flavors beautifully. The long, slow cooking results in a velvety piece of lean meat that soaks up the sweet-tart tomato sauce.

1 large beef tongue (about 2 pounds)	2 cups homemade tomato passato (page 24) or store-bought tomato puree
1 tablespoon plus 1 teaspoon kosher salt	½ cup white wine vinegar
½ cup extra-virgin olive oil	2 tablespoons sugar
1 large onion, thinly sliced	½ cup fresh parsley, chopped

Put the tongue in a pot just large enough to hold it and cover with water. Add the tablespoon of salt. Cover the pot and bring to a boil. Lower the heat and simmer until a knife can be easily inserted into the tongue with little resistance, 1½ to 2 hours, adding more water to the pot as necessary to keep the tongue covered. Remove from the pot and let cool until you can handle it, then peel the tongue—the outer membrane should come off easily. Remove the fatty parts from the lower portion of muscle (it will be striated with fat and look different from the meat of the tongue itself). Slice the tongue into ¼-inch pieces and set aside.

Heat the olive oil in a heavy pot or Dutch oven over medium heat. Add the onion and cook, stirring occasionally, until soft. Add the tomato puree, vinegar, sugar, and remaining 1 teaspoon salt and stir to combine. Lower the heat so the liquid is simmering, add the slices of tongue, and cook, partially covered, for about 45 minutes, until the liquid has reduced slightly and the tongue is very tender, stirring occasionally so the sauce does not stick to the bottom of the pan and burn.

Transfer to a serving platter and scatter parsley over. Serve warm.

BRAISED TRIPE

SERVES 4 TO 6

There are different types of tripe but the most ubiquitous is honeycomb tripe, named for its distinctive honeycomb pattern. Tripe must first be boiled, which softens it and rids it of any unpleasant odors. Once boiled, I braise it in a thick tomato sauce, as I find the acidity and saltiness of the sauce goes a long way toward smoothing out tripe's rough edges. The spongy texture of tripe contributes to its ability to soak up sauce and flavor. Serve with some grated Parmigiano-Reggiano or toss it with cooked fusilli or rigatoni.

2 pounds honeycomb tripe

6 cups water

½ cup apple cider vinegar

1 tablespoon kosher salt

2 tablespoons extra-virgin olive oil

½ cup Sofritto (page 17)

2 cups Roasted Bird Broth (page 18)

2 cups tomatoes (page 27), crushed

4 cloves garlic

2 dried bay leaves

1 (3 by 1-inch) Parmigiano-Reggiano rind

1 cup fresh Italian parsley, finely chopped

Put the tripe in a large nonreactive pot with the water, vinegar, and salt. Bring to a boil and boil gently for 1½ hours, adding water as necessary so the tripe remains covered. Remove from the water, let cool, then cut into ½-inch strips.

Heat the oil in a high-sided heavy pot over medium heat. Add the sliced tripe and cook for 5 minutes, then stir in the sofritto, broth, tomatoes, garlic, bay leaves, and Parmigiano-Reggiano rind. Turn down the heat to low and cook for 2 hours, stirring occasionally. Remove from the heat and stir in the parsley. Serve hot.

GRILLED PORK BELLY WITH ANCHOVIES

SERVES 4

This recipe is a happy accident, and its creation was based on my love for the combination of oily cured fish and rich meats, which I think always taste great together—the fish enhancing the natural umami flavors in the meat. I often toss bagna cauda (page 32) on grilled meats; this rustic recipe is another way to achieve a similar effect. Pork belly is more often braised than grilled, but grilled it becomes crispy on the edges, kissed with smoke, and as irresistible as bacon. To make slicing the raw pork belly easier, place it in the freezer for 15 minutes before slicing.

10 salt-cured anchovies

1 pound pork belly, cut crosswise into ¼-inch-thick slices

Kosher salt

2 lemons, cut into wedges

Line a plate with paper towels. Put the anchovies in a bowl and cover with cold water. Let soak for 30 minutes, then gut, pull the fillets from the skeletons, and transfer the fillets to the plate.

Season the sliced pork belly on both sides with salt and let come to room temperature. Prepare a charcoal or gas grill for direct, high-heat grilling (the grill is hot enough when you can hold your hand 1 inch above the grill grate for only 2 to 3 seconds). Put the pork belly strips on the grill and cook, turning once, until crispy on the edges and cooked through, 5 to 6 minutes.

Transfer to a plate and top each strip of pork belly with an anchovy fillet, using the back of a fork to smash the anchovy slightly so it adheres to the pork. Squeeze lemon juice over the slices and serve immediately, accompanied by more lemon wedges.

HERBED LAMB SAUSAGE

MAKES 3 POUNDS

I make this sausage in the summertime. The green herbs add a welcome freshness to the lamb—I like a mixture of basil, parsley, cilantro, and mint. The sausages can be made thick or thin, stuffed into hog or lamb casings, formed into patties, or left uncased to use as a flatbread topping or stuffing. They are great grilled, though they can also be cooked in a cast-iron pan on the stove top. I serve a pile of these, cut into short lengths with long skewers for spearing them into your mouth, as a starter. If you want to further simplify the recipe, ask your butcher to grind both the lamb and the pork belly, aiming for a 30/70 fat-to-lean ratio, then stir in the spices and finely chopped herbs.

Lamb casings for 3 pounds of meat (optional)

2 pounds boneless lamb shoulder, cut into 2-inch cubes

1 pound pork belly, cut into 2-inch cubes

1 tablespoon whole cumin seeds, coarsely ground

1 tablespoon whole coriander seeds, coarsely ground

2 teaspoons kosher salt

1 teaspoon lemon zest

2 tablespoons ice water

4 cups mixed fresh green herbs, such as parsley, mint, cilantro, and basil

---

If you're casing the sausages, prepare the casings: If the casings were packed in salt, rinse thoroughly. Place in a bowl of tepid water and soak in the refrigerator overnight. The following day, run clean water through the casings and put in a bowl. Cover with cold water and set aside.

Place the cubed meat on a rimmed baking sheet and transfer to the freezer for 30 minutes. In a medium bowl, combine the cumin, coriander, salt, lemon zest, and water.

Fill a large bowl with ice and nest a large mixing bowl into it. Grind the lamb and pork belly through the small die of a meat grinder into the bowl set in ice. Pass the herbs through the grinder into the bowl of meat. Add the spice-water mixture, then mix the herb-meat mixture well with your hands until the mixture is well combined and feels sticky.

You can leave this sausage uncased, forming it into small patties, or stuff it into casings. If casing the sausages, either twist them into links or form into small coils, securing the coils with bamboo or metal meat skewers or robust, woody lengths of rosemary that have been stripped of their leaves. For more detailed casing instructions, see the Weisswurst recipe on page 202.

Grill the sausages over indirect heat, turning as needed, until browned and cooked through (to an internal temperature of 145°F), about 10 minutes. Or preheat the oven to 300°F and cook the sausages in a cast-iron pan over medium-high heat until browned on both sides, then transfer to the hot oven and cook until the internal temperature registers 145°F, about 7 minutes.

PORK & PEPPERONCINO SAUSAGE

MAKES 3 POUNDS

I started making this sausage when I butchered my first pig at home. I worked my way through 500 pounds of pork, and by the end—exhausted, with chunks of lard literally sprinkled through my hair—I had a bucket of pig bits that were definitely edible but had been excluded from my equations of how the pig was going to come apart. I ground them up and mixed in a healthy dose of brown sugar and spice and, once I'd recovered from pork overdose and was able to eat it again, I pulled the sausage from the freezer, cooked it, and shared it with everyone who'd helped me with the butchery. It ended up being everyone's favorite, and every year after that, this spicy-sweet sausage made from all the scraps became something of a signature. I no longer butcher pigs in my kitchen, but I do still make this sausage all the time. Sausage making is easier if you have a friend helping, particularly if you're going to case the meat. This makes a reasonable-size batch, but you might consider doubling it if you want to share the spoils with your helper. If you want to simplify the recipe, ask your butcher to grind the meat for you. I use lamb casings, but hog casings will also work.

Lamb casings for 3 pounds of meat (optional)	1 tablespoon red pepper flakes
3 pounds boneless pork shoulder, cut into 1-inch cubes	1½ teaspoons fennel seeds
	½ teaspoon freshly ground black pepper
2 tablespoons ice water	3 cloves garlic, smashed to a paste
1 tablespoon brown sugar	
2 teaspoons kosher salt	

If you're planning on casing the sausages, prepare the casings: If the casings were packed in salt, rinse thoroughly. Place in a bowl of tepid water and soak in the refrigerator overnight. The following day, run clean water through the casings and put in a bowl. Cover with water and set aside.

Place the cubed meat on a rimmed baking sheet and transfer to the freezer for 30 minutes.

In a medium bowl, combine the water, brown sugar, salt, red pepper flakes, fennel seeds, black pepper, and garlic.

Nest a large mixing bowl into a bowl filled with ice. Grind the pork shoulder through the small die of a meat grinder into the bowl set in ice.

Add the water-spice mixture to the ground meat and mix with your hands until the mixture is well combined and feels sticky. Wrap tightly and refrigerate overnight.

You can leave this sausage uncased or stuff into lamb casings. If casing the sausages, either twist them into links or form into small coils. Secure the coils with strong rosemary that have been stripped of their leaves, or skewer the coils with bamboo or metal skewers and tuck in a few sprigs of rosemary. For more detailed casing instructions, see the Weisswurst recipe on page 202.

Grill the sausages over indirect heat, turning as needed, until browned and cooked through (to an internal temperature of 165°F), about 15 minutes. Or cook the sausages in a cast-iron pan over medium-high heat until browned on both sides, then transfer to a 300°F oven and cook until the internal temperature registers 165°F, about 7 minutes.

WEISSWURST

MAKES ABOUT 3 POUNDS

This sausage is creamy and light, gently spiced with ginger, lemon zest, and mace, and one of my all-time favorites. It's emulsified, which means that the meat and fat is first ground, then processed in a food processor until smooth, creating a matrix of meat and fat that gives the sausage its fine texture and its juiciness. Though the method is not difficult, for the best results you should be technically rigorous, paying attention to the temperature of the meat mixture as you process it. If it becomes too warm, the fat and meat will separate, resulting in a sausage that is dry and grainy when cooked. I like to serve this sausage in the wintertime, simply boiled and accompanied by sauerkraut and a bowl of mustard, but it's also a great sausage hot off the grill. If you want to simplify this recipe, ask your butcher to grind the meat for you.

10 feet hog casings	2 teaspoons dry mustard
1½ pounds pork belly, cut into 2-inch cubes	1½ teaspoons blanched finely minced lemon zest
¾ pound veal shoulder, cut into 2-inch cubes	1 teaspoon ground ginger
¾ pound pork shoulder, cut into 2-inch cubes	½ teaspoon mace
1½ tablespoons fine sea salt	2¾ cups (22 ounces) crushed ice
2 teaspoons sugar	¼ cup nonfat dry milk powder
2 teaspoons ground white pepper	

Prepare the casings: If the casings were packed in salt, rinse thoroughly. Place in a bowl of tepid water and soak in the refrigerator overnight. The following day, run clean water through the casings and put in a bowl. Cover with cold water and set aside.

Spread the pork belly, veal, and pork shoulder cubes in a single layer on a rimmed baking sheet and place in the freezer until stiff but not frozen solid, about 30 minutes.

Fill a large bowl with ice and nest a large mixing bowl into it. Grind the meat through the small die of the grinder, one piece at a time, into the bowl set over ice. Transfer the ground meat to the bowl of a stand mixer fitted with the paddle attachment and add the salt, sugar, white pepper, dry mustard, lemon zest, ginger, and mace. Mix on low speed until the mixture is well combined, looks homogenous, and begins to stick to the sides of the bowl.

Transfer to the refrigerator and refrigerate until very cold, 20 to 30 minutes. Put half of the meat mixture into the bowl of a food processor (leave the remaining meat mixture in the refrigerator). Add half of the crushed ice and process until the meat registers 45°F on an instant-read thermometer. Add half of the nonfat milk powder and continue processing until the mixture is very smooth and homogeneous and registers 58°F. Transfer to a bowl and refrigerate, then repeat with the remaining meat, ice, and milk powder. Combine all of the meat and mix well. Spoon 2 tablespoons of the meat mixture into a nonstick frying pan and spread into a thin patty. Cook the test patty over low heat until cooked through but not browned. Taste the sausage for seasoning and adjust as necessary.

CONTINUED

Load the meat mixture into the canister of the sausage stuffer, compressing it very lightly to remove any air bubbles. Have a clean baking sheet or two nearby, rubbed with water, as a resting place for the stuffed sausage.

Moisten the stuffer nozzle with water, then push the casing onto the nozzle, taking care not to double up on the casing. Gently begin cranking the stuffer; as soon as you see meat come out, stop and crank backward to halt the forward movement. Pull 4 to 5 inches of casing off the end of the nozzle but don't knot it. With one hand, start cranking the sausage stuffer slowly and steadily. Once the sausage starts to fill the casing, remove the air by pinching and tying a knot at the end. Your free hand should be on the casing as the sausage is being extruded, helping guide it along. Regulate the thickness of the links. If the casing feels too tight, loosen your grip on it; too loose and you can close your grip a bit; the casings should be filled but not so tight that they'll burst when twisted into links.

As the sausage comes out, arrange the filled casings in a pinwheel shape on the baking sheet. If the casing splits, cut out the damaged bit of casing and discard. Reserve the sausage that burst through the casing and add it back to the stuffer.

Beginning at the tied end of the coil, measure off a length of sausage, about 6 inches. Pinch the sausage gently to form your first link and twist forward about 7 rotations, using the palms of your hands. Form the second link, and this time pinch firmly and twist backward. Repeat this process, alternating forward and backward, until you reach the open end of the casing. Twist the open end right at the last bit of sausage to seal off the coil, and then tie a knot.

Put the sausage links on a dry baking sheet, loosely cover with plastic wrap, and place in the refrigerator overnight.

Bring a large pot of water to a boil. Add the sausages, return the water to a boil, then remove the pot from the heat and cover. Let stand 20 minutes, until an instant-read thermometer inserted into the center of the sausage registers 155°F. You can eat the poached sausages hot or transfer the sausages to an ice bath to stop the cooking, at which point the sausages can be refrigerated for up to 3 days or transferred to plastic freezer storage bags and frozen for up to 2 months. Poached weisswurst can also be grilled or pan-fried in butter over medium heat until golden brown and crisp. Serve with grainy mustard.

VITELLO TONNATO

SERVES 6

This is an unfussy dish often served in Italy during the summer, when a cold main course is welcome. The finished product is a platter of very tender, thinly sliced boiled meat covered in a flavorful tuna-caper sauce. Though it's a very traditional Italian recipe, vitello tonnato has become somewhat fashionable in the United States, often presented as some sort of a rare roast that has been thinly sliced and topped with a mayo-based sauce to which tuna and anchovy fillets have been added.

While I like that version, my own is Italian grandma–style—the meat is simmered until completely cooked through and the sauce is thickened with tuna and hard-boiled-egg yolks. The use of two types of fish in the sauce (the name means tuna-fished veal) harkens back to a time in northern Italy when salt-packed fish were used as much for salt as for flavor. Even as recently as the 1930s, many Piedmontese families could not afford the comparatively expensive granular salt and instead used salted fish as a seasoning in pretty much every sauce.

The great thing about this dish is it just keeps on giving. The cooked meat and the sauce will last a week in your fridge and any leftovers can be turned into elegant antipasto the next day or used for a great sandwich or salad topper. Though boiled meat may sound wintry, the bright, light sauce and lean cut of beef make it a dish well suited to spring and summertime. I like serving it as a first course before a nonmeaty main, like Asparagus with Fried Eggs (page 121) or a pasta with spring vegetables.

2½ pounds beef eye of round, in one piece	4 eggs
1 (750 ml) bottle dry white wine	12 ounces best-quality olive oil-packed tuna (Italian is preferable)
1 celery stalk, cut into thirds	2 tablespoons white wine vinegar
2 dried bay leaves	Juice of 1 lemon
5 fresh sage leaves	¼ cup plus 2 tablespoons extra-virgin olive oil
Kosher salt	
6 salted anchovies or 12 anchovy fillets	Fresh Italian parsley, for garnish
2 tablespoons salt-packed capers	

Trim any exterior white fat or silver skin from the eye of round and place in a large, heavy pot. Add the wine, celery, bay, sage, and a healthy pinch of salt. The meat should be fully immersed in the wine; add more wine as necessary to cover. Let sit at room temperature overnight.

Remove the bay and sage, then transfer the pot to the stove top. Bring the wine to a boil over high heat, then lower the heat so the liquid is barely simmering, cover the pot, and simmer for 1 hour. While the beef simmers, put the salt-cured anchovies in a small bowl and cover with cold water. Let soak for 30 minutes, then gut the anchovies, pull the fillets from the skeleton, and set aside. Put the capers in a separate bowl, cover with warm water, and let soak for 15 minutes, then drain, rinse in cold water, and set aside.

When the beef has cooked for an hour, uncover the pot, add the soaked anchovy fillets, and increase the heat so the liquid is simmering more vigorously. Cook for 30 minutes more, during which time the liquid should reduce by half. Remove the beef from the pot, transfer to a rimmed baking sheet, and let cool to room temperature. With a slotted spoon, remove the anchovy fillets from the broth and set aside. Save the cooking liquid.

While the beef cooks, put the eggs in a medium saucepan. Cover with cold water, then bring to a boil over high heat. Remove the pan from the heat, cover, and let stand for 9 minutes, then transfer the eggs to an ice water bath. When cool, peel the eggs and remove the yolks (the whites can be discarded or saved as a cook's snack).

In the bowl of a food processor, combine the reserved anchovy fillets, egg yolks, tuna, soaked capers, vinegar, lemon juice, and olive oil. Process until the sauce has the consistency of softly whipped cream, adding a bit of the reserved cooking liquid as necessary to achieve the correct fluffy texture but taking care not to add so much liquid that the sauce become runny. Season to taste with additional salt.

Thinly slice the cooked beef and transfer to a platter. Drizzle the sauce over, then garnish with parsley leaves. Serve at room temperature.

VEAL MEATBALLS

MAKES 30 MEATBALLS; SERVES 6

Meatballs cooked in broth end up looking like an artisan version of the IKEA favorite, enveloped in a shiny brown savory gravy, though mine—made with veal, pork, and Parmigiano-Reggiano—are way more tasty. I learned this way of cooking meatballs in northern Italy, where cooks rely less on red sauce than in southern Italy. These meatballs are light, mild, and tender and are a big hit with kids. I make them with veal when we have it from the farm, but you can substitute lean ground beef. The bread crumbs aid with texture and help the meatballs hold together, but if you omit them, you won't lose any flavor.

¼ cup dry bread crumbs	1½ teaspoons kosher salt
¼ cup milk	½ teaspoon freshly ground black pepper
1½ pounds ground veal	
½ pound ground pork	2 tablespoons extra-virgin olive oil
1 cup ground (not grated) Parmigiano-Reggiano cheese (use the punch holes of a box grater or grind in a food processor)	4 cups Roasted Bird Broth (page 18)
	1 sprig rosemary
2 eggs	1 tablespoon "OO" or all-purpose flour

In a small bowl combine the bread crumbs and milk and let stand 10 minutes, until the bread crumbs have absorbed all the milk.

In a medium bowl, combine the veal, pork, soaked bread crumbs, Parmigiano-Reggiano cheese, eggs, salt, and pepper. Mix gently but thoroughly with your hands until combined, then roll into 2-inch balls.

Heat a wide, high-sided pan over medium-high heat and add the olive oil. When the oil is hot, add the meatballs and fry, turning so they brown on all sides, until golden brown on the exterior but still raw within, about 6 minutes. Transfer the seared meatballs to a plate, pour the fat out of the pan, then deglaze the pan with the broth, using a wooden spoon to scrape up the browned bits. Return the meatballs to the pan and add the rosemary sprig. Bring the broth to a simmer and simmer for 15 minutes. Dust the tops of the meatballs with the flour, cover the pan, and let cook for 5 minutes more.

With a slotted spoon, transfer the meatballs to a warm serving dish and cover. Increase the heat so the broth is boiling and boil vigorously for 10 minutes, until the liquid has reduced and thickened some. Pour the broth over the meatballs and serve over polenta or alongside a salad.

CHICKEN BRAISED IN VINEGAR & AROMATICS

SERVES 4

Italians specialize in food that is ugly but tastes so good, and this recipe is a fine example, a study in brown. The chicken, first marinated in vinegar and wine, is then braised on the stove top in a garlicky mixture of chicken broth and anchovies, which thickens as it cooks, coating the chicken and infusing it to the bone with flavor. This is one of those simple, essential dishes that makes me love home cooking, the kind of dish that has people swiping the bottom of the bowl for extra sauce and asking for the recipe.

---

1 (3-pound) chicken, cut into 8 pieces

½ cup white wine vinegar

½ cup dry white wine

1 teaspoon kosher salt

2 tablespoons unsalted butter

2 whole salt-cured anchovies

2 cloves garlic

1 sprig rosemary

1 cup Roasted Bird broth (page 18)

In a large bowl, combine the chicken, vinegar, wine, and salt.

Melt the butter in a Dutch oven or other high-sided heavy pot over medium heat. Add the chicken and any accumulated liquid and cook, stirring occasionally, until the chicken is golden brown and all of the liquid has evaporated, about 30 minutes.

Meanwhile, put anchovies in a small bowl and add cold water to cover. Let soak for 30 minutes, then drain, gut, and pull the fillets from the skeletons. Put the anchovy fillets, garlic, rosemary leaves, and broth in a food processor or blender and process for 30 seconds. After the chicken has cooked for 30 minutes, pour this mixture over the chicken and continue to cook for 10 minutes longer, until the chicken is deeply browned and cooked through and the liquid has almost completely evaporated, coating the chicken in a thick, brown sauce. Transfer to a serving platter and serve hot.

BEER-BRAISED RABBIT WITH SHALLOTS

SERVES 6

I love braising rabbit in beer or white wine. Cooking the lean meat in liquid tenderizes it, but if you use a light-bodied beer, as I prefer, the mild flavor of the meat still comes through. If you are into those bigger bottles of artisan beer or growlers, this is a great way to use a half-fizzled bottle that is no longer drinkable. If you'd like, substitute hard cider or Prosecco for the beer. Serve this with a big salad or, if you want to echo the rabbit's diet, some cooked buttered carrots and fresh peas alongside.

1 (3-pound) rabbit, cut into 6 pieces

Kosher salt and freshly ground black pepper

Flour, for dredging

2 tablespoons unsalted butter

2 tablespoons extra-virgin olive oil

½ cup sofritto (page 17)

4 large shallots, peeled and halved

1 (12-ounce) bottle beer (I prefer brown or amber ale; avoid very hoppy beer)

1½ cups Roasted Bird Broth (page 18)

2 sprigs thyme

Season the rabbit pieces on all sides with salt and black pepper and dredge in flour to coat. Melt the butter in a large, heavy pot over medium-high heat and add the olive oil. Add the rabbit pieces and cook, turning once, until deep golden brown, about 10 minutes. Transfer to a plate.

Add the sofritto and shallots to the pan and cook, stirring, for 4 minutes, then pour in the beer. Let cook for 5 minutes, using a wooden spoon to scrape any browned bits from the bottom of the pan. Pour in the broth, add the thyme, bring the liquid to a boil, then lower the heat to medium-low and add the rabbit pieces back to the pot.

Cover the pot partially and simmer until the rabbit is very tender and the shallots are soft, 60 to 75 minutes. Transfer the rabbit pieces and shallots to a warmed platter. Increase the heat so the liquid is boiling and boil until slightly reduced, 5 minutes. Season to taste with salt and pepper. Remove the thyme sprigs and spoon the sauce around the rabbit. Serve hot.

SEARED QUAIL & HERB SALAD

SERVES 4

This is a lovely, light dinner salad: a simple combination of seared quail, herbs, and tender lettuce tossed in a bright mustardy vinaigrette. I usually buy whole quail and spatchcock them, cutting along the backbone and flattening the bird before cooking it, but if you want a more elegant presentation, a fork-and-knife affair, look for sleeve-boned quail, which are boneless save for the legs.

2 whole quail

Kosher salt and freshly ground black pepper

1 tablespoon unsalted butter

1 cup fresh parsley leaves

1 cup chervil sprigs

1 head butter or Little Gem lettuce

1 teaspoon Dijon mustard

1 tablespoon freshly squeezed lemon juice

2 tablespoons extra-virgin olive oil

Preheat the oven to 350°F. Put the quail on a work surface breast side down. With a pair of scissors or sharp knife, cut out and remove the backbone from each quail (discard or save for stock), then turn breast side up and, with the heel of your hand, press firmly on the breastbone to flatten the quails. Season on both sides with salt and pepper.

Heat a large cast-iron frying pan over high heat. When the pan is hot, add the quail, breast side down, weighting them with a second cast-iron pan or aluminum foil–wrapped brick. Sear until golden brown, 5 minutes, then flip, replace the weight, and cook on the second side for 3 minutes more. Transfer the pan to the oven and roast for 10 minutes.

Remove from the oven, transfer the quails to a plate, and top with ½ tablespoon butter each. Let cool to warm room temperature, then cut each quail into six pieces—scissors work well for this—and transfer to a large bowl. Add the parsley, chervil, and lettuce. In a small bowl, whisk together the mustard and lemon juice. Whisk in the olive oil and season to taste with salt and pepper. Pour the vinaigrette over the salad and toss with your hands to combine; season to taste with additional salt and pepper.

TWICE COOKED ORANGE DUCK

SERVES 4 TO 6

I am obsessed with crispy bird skin. It's the most delicious part, am I right? I learned this method of cooking duck from my fellow crispy skin lover and friend Angelo Garro, who starts the duck on the stove top and then finishes it in the oven. The stove-top searing, while messy business, speeds up the necessary rendering process, melting the duck's substantial subcutaneous fat and ensuring the maximum amount of crackling, golden-brown skin. I put an orange inside the bird as it roasts, a classic combination. I like the way the bright citrus flavors balance the rich gaminess of the bird. For a more pronounced citrus flavor, the roasted fruit can be squeezed on the duck just before serving.

1 (5- to 6-pound) Peking duck

1½ tablespoons kosher salt

1 blood orange, zested and quartered

1 teaspoon whole black peppercorns

1 teaspoon fennel seeds

Preheat the oven to 350°F. Season the duck all over and in the cavity with salt and let come to room temperature. Combine the orange zest, peppercorns, and fennel seeds in a spice grinder or mortar and pestle and coarsely grind. Set aside.

Put a large cast-iron pan over high heat. When the pan is very hot, add the duck and sear on all sides until the skin is golden brown and some of the fat has begun to render out from beneath the skin (this is smoky, spattery work—crank up the hood fan or open a window and put on an apron before you begin), about 10 minutes total. Transfer the duck to a plate, remove the pan from the heat, and pour off the fat from the pan, then return the duck to the pan breast side up, and sprinkle the orange zest–spice mixture over the surface and in the cavity.

Put the orange quarters in the cavity of the duck. Transfer the duck to the oven and roast until the juices run clear and an instant-read thermometer inserted into the thigh without touching bone registers 165°F, about 40 minutes.

Transfer to a serving platter. If you'd like, squeeze the roasted orange over the duck. Carve and serve.

BUTTERY SPATCHCOCKED CHICKEN

SERVES 4

I learned the value of spatchcocking—that is, removing the backbone from and gently flattening a chicken before cooking—from my friend and colleague Bronwen Hanna-Korpi. This method has the effect of increasing the surface-area-to-volume ratio, giving you two great benefits: more crispy skin and a shorter cooking time. I love the way the chicken tastes with a healthy basting of cheesy buffalo butter, but it's also great with regular butter. If you're able to salt the chicken a day in advance, it will be even juicier. If you prefer to grill the chicken instead of roasting it in the oven, see the Note at the end of the recipe.

---

1 (3-pound) chicken

2 tablespoons kosher salt

3 tablespoons buffalo milk butter or regular salted butter, at room temperature

2 lemons, cut into wedges

The night before you want to serve the chicken, place the chicken on a work surface, skin side down. With a sharp knife or a pair of poultry shears, cut down along both sides of the backbone and remove (save for making broth). Once the backbone has been removed, use the knife or scissors to remove the keel bone, the flexible wedge of cartilage at the tip of the breastbone that connects the chicken breast to the skeleton. Discard the keel bone. Flip the chicken over and open it like a book. With the heel of your hand, press firmly on the backbone to flatten the chicken.

Season the chicken on both sides with 2 tablespoons of the salt, transfer to a rimmed baking sheet, and cover loosely with plastic wrap. Refrigerate overnight. The following day, remove the chicken from the refrigerator, rinse well with cold water, and pat dry with paper towels.

Preheat the oven to 425°F. Put the chicken skin side up in a 12-inch cast-iron frying pan or roasting dish large enough to accommodate it without bending.

Dot the skin side of the chicken with the butter, then transfer to the oven and roast, basting occasionally, until the chicken skin is deep golden brown and the juices run clear when the chicken is pierced, 35 to 40 minutes. Remove from the oven and let rest 10 minutes, then cut the chicken into eight pieces and transfer to a platter. Drizzle with accumulated pan juices, season with salt, and serve with wedges of lemon.

Note: If you prefer, the chicken can also be grilled. If using charcoal, prepare your fire 30 to 45 minutes in advance; you're aiming for a medium-hot fire, meaning the coals are ready when you cannot comfortably hold your hand about 3 inches above the grill grate for more than 5 to 6 seconds. Set the grill grate on the grill (it should be about 8 inches above the bed of coals) and let preheat for 5 minutes, then put the chicken on the grate skin side down. Cut the lemons in half crosswise and lightly oil the cut surfaces. Grill the chicken for about 20 minutes, checking frequently to ensure the heat is even and the skin is not burning. Flip the chicken, add the lemons cut side down to the grill, and cook the chicken an additional 15 to 20 minutes on the second side, until the leg joint is loose and a meat thermometer inserted into the leg joint registers 160°F. Transfer to a cutting board and let rest for 10 minutes, then cut into eight pieces and serve with the grilled lemons halves.

CHICKEN-FRIED RABBIT

SERVES 4

I learned this low-and-slow frying technique from Atlanta chef Anne Quatrano, chef-owner of Bacchanalia and Star Provisions, who uses this method to make her fried chicken. During the slow fry, the naturally lean, mild rabbit meat develops that same lovely tenderness usually achieved through braising.

I soak the rabbit pieces in seasoned buttermilk before frying, which tenderizes the rabbit, and the salt penetrates down to the bone. One challenge of this recipe is how variably sized the pieces are from a parted rabbit. To correct for this, I typically stagger the frying, adding the smaller pieces of saddle and the front legs to the hot oil about 10 minutes after the larger back legs.

One great benefit of a long slow fry is that the crust remains crunchy for hours, making it a great do-ahead dish for a party or picnic. Coarse salt and a wedge of lemon are all the accompaniments the rabbit needs, but aioli (page 17) or green sauce (page 27) would also be excellent.

---

1 (2- to 3-pound) rabbit, cut into 6 pieces

3 tablespoons kosher salt

2 cups buttermilk (page 23)

Peanut or canola oil or Rendered Pork Fat (Lard) (page 21), for frying

2 cups all-purpose flour

2 tablespoons cornmeal

Sea salt, for serving

Lemon wedges, for serving

Season the rabbit pieces on all sides with 2 tablespoons of the kosher salt. Transfer to a bowl and pour the buttermilk over. Cover and refrigerate for at least 4 hours or up to overnight.

Heat 4 inches of oil in a heavy Dutch oven or pot over medium-high heat. Line a wire rack with paper towels.

While the oil heats, whisk together the flour, cornmeal, and remaining tablespoon kosher salt and transfer to a pie plate, cake pan, or rimmed plate. Remove the rabbit pieces from the buttermilk and discard the buttermilk. Working with one piece of rabbit at a time, dredge in the flour mixture, turning to coat on all sides. Transfer to a rimmed baking sheet and repeat with the remaining pieces of rabbit.

When the oil register 325°F on a deep-frying thermometer, add the largest pieces of rabbit and fry for 10 minutes, maintaining the temperature as the rabbit cooks. Add the smaller pieces of rabbit and continue frying until the crust is golden brown and crisp and the meat is cooked through, 15 minutes more (alternatively, if your pot is not large enough to accommodate all six pieces of rabbit at once, fry in two batches: larger pieces first, followed by the smaller pieces).

Transfer the fried rabbit to the rack and let drain briefly, then place on a platter. The rabbit can be served hot or at room temperature. Just before serving, sprinkle with sea salt. Serve with lemon wedges.

DUCK CONFIT

SERVES 6

This is a classic recipe that I make every autumn. It's good for a few cold-weather meals and also a nice way to ensure a supply of surplus duck fat for use in cooking brassicas like cabbage, Brussels sprouts, and cauliflower, or as a medium for roasting potatoes. You can serve whole legs of confit as an entrée, or shred the meat, crisp it in a pan, and add it to a salad. Note that confit improves with age and should be made at least 2 days before you plan to serve it, but keeps in the refrigerator for up to 3 months.

---

3 tablespoons kosher salt

1 tablespoon rubbed sage

2 teaspoons freshly ground black pepper

6 duck legs

Zest of 1 lemon, removed with a vegetable peeler

3 pounds (6 cups) duck fat, melted

In a small bowl combine the salt, sage, and black pepper. Mix to combine, then sprinkle on both sides of the duck legs. Transfer to a rimmed baking sheet and refrigerate overnight. The following day, rinse the duck legs in cold water and pat dry with paper towels.

Preheat the oven to 250°F. Transfer the duck legs to a heavy ovenproof pot or Dutch oven, add the lemon zest, and pour the melted duck fat over the legs; the legs should be completely submerged. Cover the pot and place in the oven. Cook for 3 to 4 hours, until the meat is very tender and nearly falling from the bone.

With a slotted spoon, transfer the duck legs to a clean pot or other storage vessel. Ladle the duck fat through a fine-mesh sieve over the legs, taking care to avoid the liquid that has collected at the bottom of the pot; the duck fat should completely cover the legs. Let cool completely, then cover and transfer to the refrigerator. Refrigerate for at least 2 days (or up to 3 months).

To serve the confit, remove from the refrigerator and warm over low heat until the duck fat has melted. Remove the duck legs from the fat; strain the fat and save for another use (it can be used to make another batch of confit or used with roasted potatoes or sautéed vegetables).

Heat a large cast-iron frying pan over high heat. When the pan is very hot, add the duck legs, skin side down, and cook until deeply browned, 2 to 3 minutes. Flip and cook on the second side for 2 minutes, until heated through.

SQUAB CONFIT

SERVES 4

Squab has a gamy, rich flavor, and I find that I prefer the meat either cooked quite rare or confited, which mellows its flavor and softens the texture of the meat. I like to confit squab whole, since I think it's a beautiful presentation, but you can also adapt this recipe and use halved birds.

This dish is delicious with a braised or roasted bitter green like endive, frisée, or radicchio. Like all confit, this takes several days to make, so you must plan ahead. It improves with age, though, and will keep for up to 3 months.

¼ cup kosher salt	4 whole squab
6 cloves garlic	Zest of 1 lemon, removed with a vegetable peeler
2 tablespoons fresh thyme leaves	3 pounds (6 cups) Rendered Pork Fat (Lard) (page 21), melted
12 juniper berries	

In a mortar and pestle or food processor, combine the salt, garlic, thyme, and juniper berries and pound or process into a thick paste. Slather the paste on the squabs, transfer to a rimmed baking sheet, loosely cover with plastic wrap, and let stand overnight in the refrigerator. The following day, rinse the squab in cold water and pat dry with paper towels.

Preheat the oven to 250°F. Put the squab in a heavy pot or Dutch oven large enough to accommodate the 6 birds in a single layer. Add the lemon zest to the pot, then pour the rendered pork fat over; the squabs should be submerged. Cover the pot and put in the oven. Cook for 3 to 4 hours, until the meat is tender.

With a slotted spoon, remove the squab from the lard and transfer to a clean pot. Ladle the lard over the squab, avoiding any liquid that has collected at the bottom of the pot. Let cool completely, then transfer to the refrigerator and refrigerate for at least 2 days (or up to 3 months).

When you're ready to serve the squab, remove the pot from the refrigerator and heat gently over low heat until the lard melts and you can easily pull the squabs from the fat (strain and save the fat; it can be used for another batch of confit).

Heat a dry cast-iron pan over high heat. When you see wisps of smoke rising from the pan, add the squab and sear on all sides until browned and heated through, about 5 minutes. Serve whole or use scissors to cut the birds in half.

FENNEL & BLACK PEPPER–CRUSTED PORK LOIN

SERVES 4 TO 6

I used to consider pork loin boring, usually finding the lean cut too bland. Once we started raising heritage pigs at Belcampo, my thinking changed. Ossabaw is a descendent of Ibérico pigs and the animals are quasi-feral (in addition to the feed we provide, they hunt and eat rattlesnakes on our farm). We do not raise the pure Ossabaw pigs at Belcampo, as they grow too slowly and are extremely fatty, but all of our pork has about 30 percent of the Ossabaw genes, enough to yield loins that are dark red, marbled with fat, and delicious.

The sweetness of fennel seeds complements the natural sweetness of pork. I like to make this on the grill, but it can also be roasted in the oven. If you don't have access to Ossabaw pork, look for a loin with a nice layer of fat, which will baste the meat as it cooks. This recipe is for grilling the loin, but if you prefer to oven-roast it, see the Note at the end of the recipe.

---

2 tablespoons crushed fennel seeds

1 tablespoon coarsely ground black pepper

1 tablespoon kosher salt

1 (2½- to 3-pound) boneless pork loin

In a small bowl, combine the fennel seeds, pepper, and salt. Pat the mixture onto the pork loin and let the meat come to room temperature.

Prepare a grill for indirect, medium-hot grilling. There should be a solid bed of glowing coals and you should be able to hold your hand 1 inch above the grill grate for 5 to 6 seconds. Push two-thirds of the coals to one side of the grill and spread the remaining third on the other side of the grill. Put the pork on the hottest part of the grill and cook, turning, until browned on all sides. Use a spray bottle filled with water to tame any flare-ups.

Transfer the pork to the cooler part of the grill and continue cooking, turning occasionally, until an instant-read thermometer inserted into the thickest part of the meat registers 155°F. Transfer to a rimmed plate and tent with aluminum foil. Let rest for 10 minutes, then slice into thick slices and serve.

Note: If you prefer, the pork can also be roasted. Preheat the oven to 400°F. Rub the pork with the spices and let come to room temperature as directed above. Put the pork in a roasting pan or on a rimmed baking sheet, fat side up, and transfer to the oven. Cook until the internal temperature of the roast registers 155°F on an instant-read thermometer, 45 to 55 minutes. Remove from the oven, tent with foil, and let rest for 10 minutes, then slice into thick slices and serve.

THE GREATEST PORK SPARERIBS

SERVES 4

Pork spareribs are a go-to staple for any time I am looking for a meaty main course that will reheat and hold well at room temperature. It's also very easy to do this recipe in stages: make the rub and season the meat one day and cook it one or two days later. I find cumin, brown sugar, paprika, and garlic are essential pork rub ingredients. Beyond that, you have a lot of flexibility. Grate in some nutmeg, add a spoonful of harissa, or experiment with other dried spices. When buying pork spareribs, look for ones with some visible fat on the outside of the ribs—it's a lot easier to trim off a little extra fat than to add it back on! The fat will dissolve slowly as the ribs cook, basting the meat so the ribs don't dry out. If you can only find really lean ribs, you can drape the rubbed rack with a few strips of bacon. These are great served with the Caramelized Apples (page 268).

---

1 tablespoon paprika

2½ teaspoons whole coriander seeds

2½ teaspoons whole cumin seeds

1½ teaspoons whole black peppercorns

3 dried bay leaves

1½ tablespoons kosher salt

½ cup light brown sugar

1 (3-pound) rack pork spareribs

2 tablespoons red wine vinegar

2 cloves garlic, minced

In a mortar and pestle or spice grinder, combine the paprika, coriander seeds, cumin seeds, peppercorns, and bay leaves and finely grind. Transfer to a bowl and add the salt and brown sugar.

Rub the mixture onto the ribs, coating both sides, then transfer to a rimmed baking sheet, loosely cover with plastic wrap, and refrigerate overnight.

Preheat the oven to 350°F and line a baking sheet with aluminum foil.

Combine the vinegar and garlic in a small bowl. Brush any loose spice rub from the ribs, then rub the racks with the vinegar mixture and transfer to the baking sheet, bone side down.

Bake until the ribs are deeply colored and very tender but not yet falling from the bone, about 1½ hours, occasionally rotating the pan to encourage even cooking. Transfer the cooked ribs to a cutting board and use a sharp knife to cut between each rib. Serve warm.

WINE-BRAISED BRISKET

SERVES 6

Brisket can be a bit of a beast—the cut is large, with a lot of intramuscular fat, and it has big stringy fibers due to its placement on the animal: it's part of the animal's pectoral muscles, those big strong chest muscles that support the animal's head and shoulders.

I love the flavor of brisket, but I do not like when it's cooked so long it breaks down into a big pile of pulled beef swamped in liquefied tallow. My style of cooking it—first searing the brisket, then braising it at a low temperature for a long time before finally returning it to the oven to recrisp the crust—is a three-step process that pays dividends: a very tender brisket with a nicely browned exterior that can be sliced into nice pieces without falling apart.

The slices can then be served in the flavorful cooking liquid, once it has been defatted; use any leftovers for making sandwiches.

4 pounds beef brisket	2 whole cloves
Kosher salt and freshly ground black pepper	4 juniper berries
1 red onion, cut into eighths	1 teaspoon whole black peppercorns
2 sprigs rosemary	1 (750 ml) bottle dry red wine

Preheat the oven to 300°F. Put the brisket on a work surface and trim some of the visible fat cap. Season generously on both sides with salt and pepper.

Heat a large cast-iron frying pan over high heat. When the pan is very hot, add the brisket fat side down and sear until deep golden brown, 5 to 6 minutes. Flip the brisket and sear on the second side until brown.

Transfer the brisket to a roasting pan and add the onion, rosemary, cloves, juniper berries, and peppercorns. Pour in the wine, then add enough water so that the liquid reaches halfway up the side of the brisket. Cover the pan with aluminum foil, transfer to the oven, and cook for 4 hours, until the brisket is tender but not falling apart; you want to be able to slice it, not shred it.

Remove the pan from the oven and carefully transfer the brisket to a rimmed baking sheet. Increase the oven temperature to 375°F. Pour the braising liquid through a fine-mesh sieve into a measuring cup. Return the meat to the oven for 20 minutes, until a dark brown crust has formed on the top.

Transfer the brisket to a cutting board and cut against the grain into ½-inch-thick slices. Skim and discard any fat that's risen to the top of the braising liquid and season to taste. If the braising liquid is too thin for your liking, transfer to a small saucepan and bring to a boil; boil until thickened and reduced. Put the sliced brisket on a platter and spoon some of the braising liquid over. Serve warm.

BEEF INVOLTINI WITH HAM & PROVOLONE

MAKES 20 INVOLTINI; SERVES 6

I first tasted this dish when visiting a farm in the area around Modica, Sicily. In that region, like many of the poorer areas of rural Europe, there are not specific breeds of beef, each with its specific purpose. Instead, the cows are used as tractors, as milk producers, and, once their other functionalities are exhausted, slaughtered and eaten. Long story short: tough meat.

One great way to compensate for its toughness is to slice it thin and cook it a long time, as is done in these involtini, a dish that's popular in the region. I make these out of thin slices of beef top round or eye of round, those big load-bearing muscles in the fore- and hindquarters of the cow. They are a little fussy to roll up and pin together, but once they've been assembled they are surprisingly robust, and after a long, slow braise they become tender little packages with a soft, cheesy filling. These are also awesome reheated the next day and used in place of a meatball in a hot sandwich.

2½ pounds beef eye of round	Kosher salt and freshly ground black pepper
1½ cups fresh bread crumbs	2 teaspoons dried rosemary
⅓ cup fresh Italian parsley, chopped	⅓ cup extra-virgin olive oil
2 small yellow onions, finely chopped (about 1½ cups)	2 tablespoons tomato paste
10 thin slices prosciutto cotto (cooked Italian ham), cut in half crosswise	4 cups homemade tomato passato (page 24) or store-bought tomato puree
10 thin slices provolone, cut in half	1 tablespoon all-purpose flour
	6 small sprigs fresh rosemary

Place the beef in the freezer for 20 minutes.

In a medium bowl, combine the bread crumbs, parsley, and half of the chopped onion.

Remove the beef from the freezer and, with a very sharp knife, thinly slice into twenty slices, each about 2 ounces. Working with one slice of meat at a time, use a meat mallet or rolling pin to pound the slice to a thickness of ¼ inch. Repeat with the remaining slices.

Put a piece of pounded meat on a work surface and top with a piece of prosciutto and a piece of provolone. Place a generous spoonful of the bread crumb mixture on top of the prosciutto and cheese, then roll the meat around the filling like a cigar and secure the roll with a toothpick. Repeat until all the involtini have been rolled. Season with salt, black pepper, and dried rosemary.

Heat the olive oil in a large sauté pan over medium-high heat. Add the rolls and brown on all sides, about 7 minutes, then transfer to a rimmed plate. In the now-empty sauté pan, add the remaining chopped onion and the tomato paste (if the pan is dry, add another tablespoon of oil). Lower the heat to medium-low and cook, stirring, for 2 minutes. Pour in the tomato puree and, with a wooden spoon, dislodge any browned bits from the bottom of the pan. Add the involtini to the tomato sauce, arranging the rolls so that they poke out of the sauce, and sprinkle the flour over the visible parts of the involtini.

Bring the tomato puree to a boil. Lower the heat to medium-low, cover the pan partially, and cook until the beef is very tender, about 1 hour 20 minutes. After the involtini have cooked for 15 minutes, turn the involtini with tongs often to prevent them from

sticking to the bottom of the pan; the sauce will have begun to thicken and you do not want it to scorch.

Remove the pan from the heat and let the involtini rest in the sauce for 30 minutes before serving, then transfer to a warmed serving platter and remove the toothpicks from each roll. Season the tomato sauce to taste with additional salt and pepper. It should be thick; if it's too thin, reduce it over medium heat, stirring often. Spoon a few cups of sauce over the involtini, garnish with the fresh rosemary sprigs, and serve hot, with the remaining sauce in a bowl alongside.

ROAST BEEF WITH HORSERADISH-WALNUT SAUCE

SERVES 8

I am a champion of inexpensive roasts. In part, this is a political agenda; for both my business and my beliefs, I encourage people to eat a broader range of cuts of meat, not just the prestigious prime middle meats from the animal's rib section. Living in northern Italy all those years, I also became accustomed to the lean, flavorful cuts from the big continental breeds of cow.

What I've learned over the years of cooking eye of round and top round as roasts is that it's a bit more finicky than a prime rib roast, which has enough fat to be a bit more forgiving, but it compensates for any fat shortcomings with its deep, beefy flavor. To ensure a perfect roast, always bring the meat to room temperature and salt it a day before you plan to cook it, then cook it at a lower temperature and for slightly less time than you think it needs. I find with these leaner cuts the residual heat, or carryover cooking, has a more pronounced effect, and overcooking will truly ruin the roast.

If serving the roast hot from the oven, I like to pair it with a rich and delicious sauce—you could go with a classic béarnaise, of course, or try the creamy walnut sauce spiked with nose-clearing horseradish. Cold roast beef is great dressed with bagna cauda (page 32) or green sauce (page 27).

1 (4-pound) eye of round roast, tied with butcher's twine into a tight cylinder

2 tablespoons kosher salt

1 teaspoon freshly ground black pepper

2 tablespoons Rendered Beef Fat (Tallow) (page 22) or canola oil

1 sprig rosemary

Flaky salt, such as Maldon, for serving

Horseradish-Walnut Sauce (recipe follows), for serving

Remove the meat from the refrigerator, season all over with kosher salt and pepper, and let the meat come to room temperature. Depending on the temperature of the roast and the room, this may take up to a few hours.

Preheat the oven to 225°F. Heat a cast-iron griddle or your largest frying pan over high heat. Add the tallow, and when the tallow is hot, sear the roast on all sides until well browned.

Transfer to a roasting pan or rimmed baking sheet, sprinkle with rosemary leaves, and roast for 1 hour 15 minutes, or until a meat thermometer inserted into the center of the roast registers 135°F. Remove from the oven, tent the meat loosely with aluminum foil, and let rest for 20 minutes.

Remove the butcher's twine and thinly slice the beef with a sharp knife. Transfer to a platter, sprinkle with flaky salt, and serve with Horseradish-Walnut Sauce.

HORSERADISH-WALNUT SAUCE

¼ cup walnuts

2 tablespoons grated fresh horseradish

4 green onions, sliced

1 cup full-fat yogurt (not Greek)

½ cup mayonnaise or aioli (page 17)

Kosher salt and freshly ground black pepper

Freshly squeezed lemon juice

In a food processor, whiz together the walnuts, horseradish, and green onions until the walnuts are finely chopped. Add the yogurt and mayonnaise and whiz just until combined. Transfer to a bowl and season to taste with salt and pepper and lemon juice. Serve alongside the roast beef or use as a spread for roast beef sandwiches.

RACK OF GOAT OR LAMB

SERVES 4

Cooking a whole rack is the best way to prepare chops for a crowd, because searing individual chops at the last minute can be difficult to execute if you have dinner guests and can lead to inconsistencies in doneness. The challenge when cooking the whole rack is getting enough of a sear on the exterior of the rack to get all of that delicious umami flavor without overcooking the meat.

When grilling goat or lamb racks, I cook them over indirect heat until the internal temperature indicates they're nearly done, then I move them over to the hotter part of the grill and quickly sear the exterior. When cooking indoors, as per the recipe below, it's easier to get a nice sear on the whole rack in a cast-iron pan and then finish in the oven. This is a spectacular dish to serve family-style, either carved tableside or with the rack separated into chops in the kitchen, then piled high on a cutting board alongside a big bowl of chimichurri (page 28). I never buy frenched racks of lamb, because I like to nibble on the bits of meat and fat around the ribs.

---

1 rack goat or lamb chops (about 2 pounds)

Kosher salt

Chimichurri (page 28), for serving (optional) or chopped parsley

---

Preheat the oven to 400°F. With the point of a paring knife, score the shiny white silver skin covering the rib bones, crisscrossing the silver skin with a grid of scores about ½ inch wide. Salt the rack generously on all sides and let the meat come to room temperature.

Heat a large cast-iron frying pan over high heat until it's smoking hot. Add the rack to the pan, fat side down, using tongs to press the exterior of the meat against the pan, rotating it as necessary until it's a deep walnut brown all over.

Transfer the pan to the oven and roast for 15 minutes, until an instant-read thermometer inserted into the thickest part of the rack registers 120°F.

Remove the pan from the oven, transfer the chops to a cutting board, tent with aluminum foil, and let stand for 10 minutes (the temperature will rise to 125°F to 130°F for medium-rare while the meat rests). Cut between the rib bones into individual chops and serve immediately, accompanied by chimichurri or chopped parsley.

SIMPLE SEARED BEEF HEART

SERVES 4 TO 6

Beef heart is a flavorful muscle that is extremely lean and deeply beefy, with a chewy texture and flavor similar to hanger steak. But unlike steak, it's versatile enough that it can be quickly cooked over high heat—my preference—or stewed for a long time until tender.

---

1 (2-pound) beef heart

2 teaspoons kosher salt

Extra-virgin olive oil, for serving

Flaky salt, such as Maldon, for serving

Chimichurri (page 28), optional for serving

Trim all of the white fat from the exterior of the heart. Pull the heart open with your hands and cut it along the thinnest part to divide it into two portions.

Heat a cast-iron pan over high heat. When the pan is smoking hot, add the heart and sear on one side, pressing down hard on the meat so it forms a nice dark crust, about 3 minutes. Because heart is so lean, it won't sear in the same way a steak does; it will seem as if it's just slightly drying out. Flip the heart and cook on the second side for 3 to 5 minutes more, until medium-rare. It's a bit challenging to tell if heart is done, as the meat is quite resilient and bouncy to begin with. That said, heart is so much less juicy than steak, so cutting into it to check the doneness won't cause it to dry out the way a steak might if you did the same.

When the heart is cooked, pull from the pan and let rest for 7 or 8 minutes, then thinly slice, drizzle with olive oil, and sprinkle with flaky salt. Serve the chimichurri alongside.

GRILLED SWEETBREADS

SERVES 4

I learned to love sweetbreads in South America, where they are served as a starter, crisp and hot off the grill. In the United States, we usually see sweetbreads—the thymus gland of a cow—breaded and fried, which enhances the organ's naturally fatty, rich flavor. In grilling, that richness is downplayed as the sweetbreads lose fat when slowly cooked over coals and in turn absorb a smokiness that contrasts nicely with the flavor and soft consistency of the organ meat. During the long cooking time, the exterior of the sweetbreads gets deeply browned while the interior remains juicy. It's my favorite way to prepare them, garnished only with flaky salt and a squeeze of lemon.

4 whole beef sweetbreads, about 12 ounces (approximately 3 ounces each)	1 teaspoon kosher salt
	1 lemon
	Flaky salt, such as Maldon

Season the sweetbreads with kosher salt and let stand at room temperature for 1 hour.

Prepare a grill for direct, medium-hot grilling (about 300°F; you can hold your hand 3 to 4 inches above the grill grate for 5 to 6 seconds). Put the sweetbreads directly onto the grill grate—they will stick at first but once they begin to brown they will easily detach from the grate. Grill, turning occasionally, until deeply browned on both sides and compact, reduced in size by almost half, about 40 minutes.

Remove the sweetbreads from the grill and transfer to a cutting board. Let rest for just a minute or two, until they are cool enough to handle, then cut crosswise into 1-inch slices. Squeeze some lemon juice over the slices and sprinkle with flaky salt. Serve immediately.

A steak primer

As a child, I can recall eating a steak only once: with my grandfather on a trip to Monterey. We went to a really classic American restaurant, and my grandfather, sensing a gap in my culinary experience, made a point of ordering me a T-bone.

My parents explained the lack of meat consumption during my childhood as a holdover from their ten years living in Bavaria with hardly any extra cash (at the time, my mom was a goldsmith, my dad a researcher). They couldn't afford red meat and learned to live without it. I think it was also a statement for them—they were both the products of very traditional 1950s homes where their moms made red meat every night with veggies from a can. Their rebellion, such as it was, entailed growing a big garden and serving spaghetti for dinner, with the occasional chicken. I am a child of the 1980s and '90s, so the fat- and cholesterol-related paranoia of the era was certainly a factor in our red meat–free diet as well.

I began cooking and eating red meat in my twenties in Italy, starting with braises and *carne cruda*, and only really began cooking steaks in my thirties when I started buying meat direct from a California farm and then had oodles of aged, marbled cuts in my freezer. Not having the economic pressure of ruining an expensive cut (that's the beauty of prepaying for a massive amount of meat: you don't realize, in the moment, how much money you wasted by screwing up dinner), I began experimenting with cooking steak and started to develop my technique.

I later spent a year or so working on a consulting gig that took me to Uruguay, land of carnivores, and during that time I learned how to burn down wood to coals and cook my steaks over the open fire, a practice that I continue today when I'm on the Belcampo farm and which can be replicated at home by using good wood charcoal in place of accelerant-soaked charcoal briquettes. Cooking meat over a glowing bed of coals can't be beat, and the flavor of the finished meat (and the experience itself) can't be replicated on a gas grill. For a Sunday afternoon activity, I like nothing more than making a big fire, watching it burn down, and then cooking big pieces of meat on it— so I guess you can say I have come full circle from my steak-free childhood.

The definitive recipe for how to cook a steak is as much—or more—about your interaction with the beef and the technique involved in cooking it than it is about precisely measuring a certain amount of salt to rub on it. Here are a few key details about selecting and preparing steak.

Choosing your meat

My favorite steaks are bone-in New York strip steaks and bone-in rib-eyes. The techniques below work equally well for a T-bone, porterhouse, or sirloin tip. For these middle-meat cuts, I always choose a steak that has been dry-aged, as I find it makes the texture of the cooked cut creamier and better. I eat exclusively grass-fed and grass-finished beef (for more on this, see page 238). Don't worry if there is a little bit of dark red exterior on the meat; this is a result of the meat being exposed to the air during aging. You can cut it off if you'd like, but it will just get all dark and crispy and delicious when cooked, so I usually leave it.

I have my steaks cut a maximum of 1½ inches thick. Though thicker steaks have great shelf appeal, I find that they're impossible to cook properly over coals unless you're willing to first cook the steak sous vide, which I think impacts the juiciness and flavor and is impractical for most home cooks. With a 1½-inch cut, you have the right surface-area-to-volume ratio to get a dark, delicious sear on the exterior without overcooking the interior. Too much thinner and the interior gets overcooked, much thicker and it remains cold and bloody.

I never cut the fat cap off my raw steak, even if it's abundant. I don't eat it either, but I find it really shields the edge of the steak and makes that part of the meat cook more evenly, and it can easily be trimmed once the meat has been cooked.

I buy one steak for every two people I am serving. Our steaks from Belcampo are big—we kill our beef almost a year older than conventional operations—but this is also a reflection of how I like to serve it. I like to cut the steak off the bone tableside and slice it into thick slices, steakhouse-style. I find that most people are satisfied with three or four thick slices of steak, especially if you're serving other dishes. If you serve everyone a whopping whole steak—unless you're hosting a crowd of extreme eaters—you end up with a lot of expensive leftovers. Another nice outcome of this tableside carving approach is that you and your guests can select the more rare, medium, and well-done portions of the steak according to preference.

I take my steaks out of the refrigerator in the morning before I leave for work and rub them with salt. I like kosher salt, mineral salt, or sea salt. I use a healthy pinch on each side and rub the bone and the fat cap with it as well—about a scant teaspoon per side for mineral or sea salt and a full teaspoon for kosher. I don't recommend iodized table salt.

I let the steak rest at room temperature, salted, all day long, because I find it most convenient to do so, but this process can be condensed to about 3 hours if you are short on time. Obvious food safety note: If you live in a hot climate without air conditioning and the daytime temperature exceeds 70°F, don't leave the steak out all day, just a few hours. If you are unable to get the steak salted and to room temperature the slow way, put it in a plastic ziptop storage bag and run warm water over the meat for 15 minutes, then salt it. The meat will have a little less salt penetration, but other than that, it will be nearly indistinguishable from the one that's rested all day.

Cooking your steak

My instructions below are for cooking medium-rare. If you are looking for well-done, double all the times suggested below.

My default method for cooking steak when I don't have time to build a fire is pan-frying it in a searing-hot cast-iron pan. I put the cast-iron pan on the hottest burner and let it sit on the heat for at least 3 minutes and up to 5 minutes until it's screaming hot. When the pan is hot, add the steak and sear for 2 minutes, 1 minute on each side, and—holding the steak upright with your tongs—spend about 2 minutes more searing all of the edges of the steak: the fat cap, the bone, and any red exposed flesh on the sides of the steak.

Then turn the heat off under the pan and let your steak rest in the pan for another minute on each side. When I am cooking a bone-in steak, I increase this rest time to 2 minutes on each side, as the presence of the bone slows down the rapidity of heat transfer within the meat, and the extra minute helps ensure that meat nearest the bone is not raw-rare. Then I pull the steaks out of the pan, transfer them to a cutting board, invert the cast-iron pan over the steaks, and let rest for 10 minutes. I can fit two big steaks in one large cast-iron pan; if I am doing four steaks, I use my cast-iron griddle set across two burners. You have to move the steaks more frequently in that scenario, as on most stoves one burner is hotter, but the results and timing are equivalent.

When I am cooking over an open fire, I begin by lighting my wood about 4 hours before I want to start cooking. If using hardwood charcoal, I light it about 1 hour before I want to cook. In both cases, I start with a big fire so that when it burns down there will be a generous bed of coals. The key technique for cooking steak over the coals is to create three gradations of heat, which you accomplish by piling and spreading the coals. On one side of the grill, I pile about two-thirds of the coals to create the hottest area, what I call the Sear Zone. In this area of your grill, you should not be able to stand the heat if you hold your hand 1 inch above your grill grate. I pull the remaining third of the coals over to create the second hottest area, or Cooking Zone, which should be about 100°F cooler than the Sear Zone, meaning you can hold your hand 1 inch above the grill grate for 2 to 3 seconds. The third area is just the edge of the grill, with few, if any, coals beneath it. I think of it as the Chill-Out Zone, where the meat can relax before and after cooking.

As I am getting my coals raked out and organizing the grill, I set my steaks in the Chill-Out Zone to come to temperature. They can hang out there for an hour. Twenty minutes before I plan to serve the steaks, I move them to the Sear Zone and let them sizzle for about 2 minutes on each side, using tongs to get a crusty sear on the bone side (if bone-in) and fat cap as well. I then move the steaks to the Cooking Zone, where they cook for 2 to 3 minutes on each side. I know the steaks are ready when the resilience of their flesh (when I poke them with my finger) is akin to poking the skin on my hand between my thumb and my forefinger when I am making a fist. At that point, I move the steaks back to the coolest part of the Chill-Out Zone. If it's a cold and windy day, you can tent them on the grill with a little aluminum foil. After about 5 minutes of resting on the grill, transfer them to your serving board and let rest for another 5 minutes or so.

Serving your steak

If you are slicing your steak tableside, do so at the last minute before serving so it does not get cold. Given the amount of marbling in a good, dry-aged New York or rib-eye steak, I typically find they don't need much in the way of garnish. However, a nice pat of butter on each steak is a great touch. Add it right when you transfer the meat to the cutting board, a good 5 minutes before you slice it so it has time to melt and mix with the meaty juices on the board. Sometimes I tuck a few sprigs of rosemary around the cooked steaks, which gently perfumes the meat, and I always serve steak with a bowl of flaky salt alongside, so everyone can season the meat to their liking.

The taste of meat

I prefer the taste of grass-fed and grass-finished beef to corn-fed. I also like eating grass-fed meat because I know that it's healthier for me, for the animals, and for the planet. Raising beef exclusively on grass is a guiding principle of my company, Belcampo; I believe it's the right thing to do.

But it's not just about my beliefs—there is a lot of science to back up the health and environmental claims of my dogma. On the flavor side, however, there has been a chorus of dissent about the taste of meat fed and finished on grass, as compared to conventional corn-finished meat. I suspect that grass-fed meat got much of its bad reputation in the early days, when the farmers producing that product were cash flow–constrained and often butchering/processing carcasses before the animals were in the right physical condition for market. Add to that the fact that these small ranchers were often working with huge industrial slaughterhouses, where a few minutes on a stressful kill floor could undo two years of careful work in raising the animal (stress during slaughter can cause the animal's meat to toughen and darken). But the techniques—both in raising and in processing grass-fed beef—have developed over time, and it's my belief that much of the grass-fed meat available now is as flavorful as anything corn-fed or corn-finished, with the added ethical and environmental benefits.

Imagine that you ate exclusively spinach. Now imagine you ate exclusively Fritos. Obviously, you would gain weight faster if you consumed only corn chips, and cattle are no different. When they eat only grass they take up to a year longer to reach sexual maturity, and it's sexual maturity that triggers the animal's production of intramuscular fat (cows, like people, get fatter after puberty).

At Belcampo, we are working to redeem the flavor of grass-fed and finished beef. The main way we are doing that is by slaughtering animals when they're older—around twenty-eight months compared to eighteen months for most mainstream operations—when they have developed much more fat (despite their all-grass diet). Being older, their beefy flavor is more pronounced, and thanks to a really calm, clean slaughtering process (which we control every step of, since we now own our own slaughterhouse near the farm), doesn't turn gamy but instead remains deliciously beefy. I like that rich flavor—it makes everything from braises to steaks more complex and satisfying.

About aging beef

Dry-aging beef is achieved when a carcass is hung in climate-controlled conditions with high humidity for anywhere from a few days to as long as a year. The ideal amount of aging time for beef varies greatly from cut to cut.

The most important factors in the length of aging are the ratio of surface area to volume and the nature of the surface of the beef. An unskinned half beef can age for up to a year because it has a relatively low surface-area-to-volume ratio and all of its exposed surfaces are covered with leather, fat cap, or bones—all relatively impermeable surfaces. On the other extreme, a trimmed skirt steak or flap steak could dry-age for only a couple of days because it has a high surface-area-to-volume ratio and all of its exposed surfaces are highly permeable meat.

A tertiary factor is that the fattier a piece of beef is, the longer it needs to age before the effects are noticeable and the longer it can be aged. This is due to the relative difficulty that microbes have in piercing through intramuscular fat with its "root systems" compared to piercing through lean meat with its relatively high moisture and pliable cell walls. When you read about those 100-day aged steaks, they are always a big fatty rib-eye and never a lean eye of round.

The vast majority of American beef is "wet-aged." For wet-aging, meat is vacuum-sealed in plastic to preserve it for transport or resale. Slaughterhouses and retailers like to upsell this transport and storage time, calling it aging, but because the plastic doesn't allow the meat to breathe and keeps it in contact with its own blood, the meat can often develop a sour flavor, nothing like the rich, deep flavor that comes with careful dry-aging.

Dry-aging, by contrast, allows the water in meat to evaporate, thus increasing the meat's perceived "beefiness," since there is proportionally less water to muscle fiber. This dehydration makes any defects in the product more noticeable: it exaggerates and concentrates flavor. So, if your beef started out with a gamy flavor when fresh, when it ages, it can taste harsh and livery as those flavors concentrate and mature. This evaporation also effectively increases the price of dry-aged beef, which can lose between 15 and 40 percent of its total weight during aging. Since beef is sold by weight, this loss in water directly translates to money.

There is also an important microbial function occurring while the water evaporates: long, threadlike mycelia of various airborne fungi act upon the meat muscle fibers. These microbes do not cause spoilage; they actually work against it by forming an external "crust" on the meat's surface, which is trimmed off when the meat is prepared for cooking. These fungal species complement the natural enzymes in the beef by helping tenderize and increase the flavor of the meat. They also increase the natural probiotic content of your meat, making it essentially a "live" food—hell, it's as healthy as sauerkraut!

Dry-aging beef is among the most amazing processes in food, where microbes do the work of a prep cook, making your ingredients perfect for consumption. It sits alongside ripening cheese, malting barley, and fermenting grapes in the book of processes that take advantage of the microbiome to make food taste better and improve its digestibility. These microlevel processes also mean we end up with more complexity of savory, sweet, and umami flavors. My friend food scientist Harold McGee says it best: "There's no cooking method that can generate the depth of flavor of a dry-aged piece of meat."

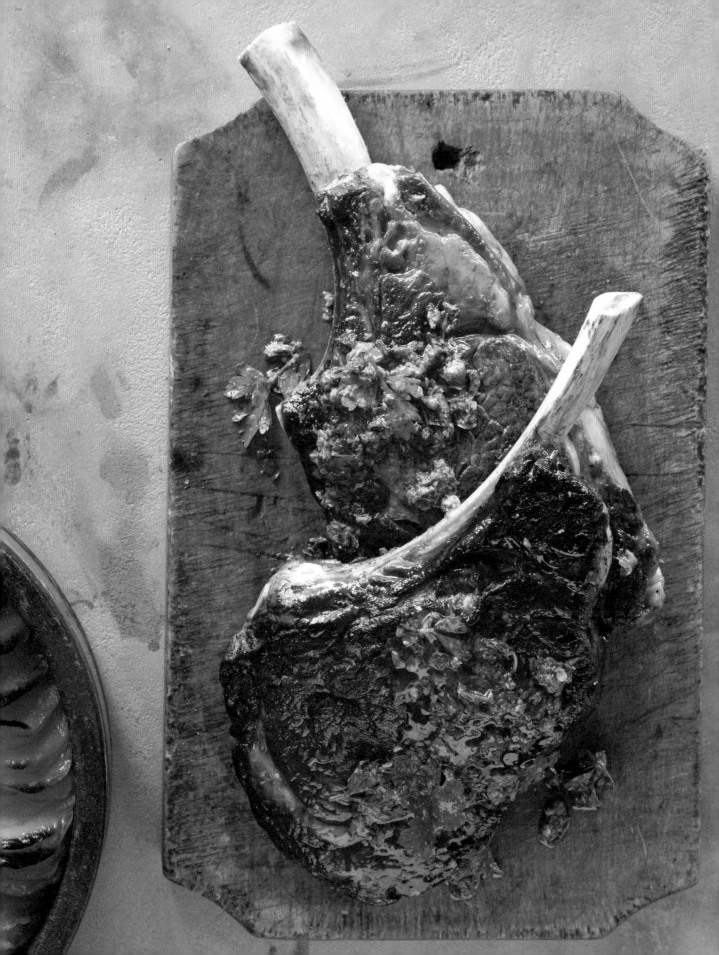

STAY A WHILE

DESSERTS

DESSERTS

I had a brief career as a baker when I was younger, long enough to recognize that the precision and exactitude required in baking was not for me. From that time, I retained a few go-to recipes that I like for their simplicity and because they can be made in advance. My preference is for sweets that are not too sweet: simple custards, like a tangy buttermilk panna cotta; fruit-based desserts, including a bracing lemon granita or jam tartlets topped with crème fraîche and a spoonful of tart apricot jam; and simple cookies that I can dip in coffee or wine. The benefit of these gently sweet desserts is that any leftovers are great for breakfast the next day.

But even though elaborate desserts may not be my forte, I understand and appreciate that every meal needs a nice conclusion. Oftentimes, I'll break out some good chocolate and serve it with nuts and dried fruit or serve a favorite cheese with some preserves alongside. I also love to make simple cookies and serve a pile of them next to a bowl of mandarin oranges or tangerines, dates, or other seasonal fruit. Add a glass of vin santo or an old spirit served neat, and it's a perfect ending.

PANFORTE

MAKES ONE 10-INCH PANFORTE

Panforte is an ancient energy bar. The name literally means "strong bread" in Italian, and it originated in the port town of Genova, baked for sailors who would take it on their journeys, preventive medicine against scurvy as well as a dense, nutrient-packed foodstuff.

The original recipe was made from honey cooked down to increase its sugar level mixed with honey-candied fruits and nuts. The modern version has a portion of sugar in addition to the honey (which also cuts about 3 hours off the cooking time, I'd estimate) and a bit of flour, to make it sliceable.

This traditional sweet is true to its origins in that it improves dramatically with age. I make a few rounds of this right after Thanksgiving every year and then slowly chip away at it as a snack and an easy dessert through the spring. I like to give it a month to age before eating it. The texture improves and the spicing gets more complex and interesting. My version of panforte is California-fied, with the addition of high-quality dried fruit to a base of candied orange and citron.

You can vary the proportion of candied and dried fruit, although I would not recommend eliminating the candied fruit entirely; it adds body and signature flavor to the panforte. Even if you have fruitcake-related trauma in your past, it's an essential ingredient here, so don't omit it. Make sure you buy fresh, large pieces of candied orange peel and citron—the prechopped variety is often dried out. For the dried fruit, using sulfured fruits is a must, and tart dried fruit, like dried Blenheim apricots or sour cherries, should make up about half the total volume of dried fruit.

I always use a silicone cake pan to make this dish. If you do not have a silicone pan, I highly suggest you borrow or purchase one prior to making this, as panforte is extremely sticky and this pan makes unmolding the finished cake much easier. Panforte will keep, tightly wrapped in plastic, for up to a year in the refrigerator. If you are storing it at room temperature, I recommend vacuum-sealing it in plastic to increase its longevity.

---

3 cups whole peeled hazelnuts

3 cups whole blanched almonds

Edible wafer paper

1½ pounds (24 ounces) mixed dried fruit (a mixture of peaches, apricots, nectarines, tart cherries, figs, and prunes)

¾ pound (12 ounces) candied citron

¾ pound (12 ounces) candied orange peel

1 cup all-purpose flour

2 tablespoons cocoa powder

2 teaspoons ground cinnamon

1 teaspoon nutmeg

1 teaspoon ground allspice

1 teaspoon kosher salt

½ teaspoon ground cloves

2¼ cups granulated sugar

1¼ cups honey

2 cups confectioners' sugar

Preheat the oven to 350°F. Spread the hazelnuts and almonds on two baking sheets and bake in the oven until lightly toasted, 10 to 15 minutes, watching carefully so the nuts don't burn.

Line a 10-inch round silicone cake pan with wafer paper.

With a lightly oiled knife, cut all the dried fruit, citron peel, and orange peel into small pieces. (Alternatively, you can chop the dried and candied fruit in the food processor in batches; add some flour and cocoa powder to each batch to prevent the fruit from sticking together.)

CONTINUED

In a large bowl, whisk together the flour, cocoa powder, cinnamon, nutmeg, allspice, salt, and cloves. Add the chopped dried fruit and nuts and toss to coat.

In a large saucepan over medium-high heat, combine the granulated sugar and honey. Bring to a boil and cook until the mixture registers 238°F to 240°F on a candy thermometer. Immediately pour the hot syrup over the dried fruit mixture and, with a lightly oiled metal spoon, mix quickly and thoroughly.

Transfer the mixture to the silicone pan and use the back of the spoon to spread evenly. Lightly moisten your hands and press the mixture firmly and evenly to compact it as much as possible. Bake the panforte until the edges appear matte and the center is still soft but no longer sticky, about 50 minutes.

Transfer to a wire rack and let cool for 15 minutes. Spread half of the confectioners' sugar onto a rimmed baking sheet and unmold the panforte onto the baking sheet. Sprinkle the remaining confectioners' sugar over the top of the panforte and use your fingers to rub it into the top and bottom surfaces and sides of the panforte to coat. Let stand overnight. Though the panforte can be eaten the next day, it improves upon sitting, and will taste even better after it has sat for a week (or up to a year). Wrap very tightly in several layers of plastic wrap and store in the refrigerator until ready to serve; it will keep for up to 6 months. To serve, cut into very thin wedges.

AMARETTI MORBIDI

MAKES 3 DOZEN COOKIES

Amaretti are a classic Italian cookie made primarily from almond flour. The versions available commercially are typically very dry. I love the softer texture of homemade amaretti, which have a slight crust on the outside and a dense, chewy center.

2 cups almond flour	2 egg whites
1 cup sugar	Pinch of salt
2 tablespoons all-purpose flour	½ teaspoon almond extract

Sift the almond flour, sugar, and all-purpose flour into a large bowl.

Using a stand mixer fitted with the whisk attachment, beat the egg whites with the salt until they form soft peaks. Whisk in the almond extract, then pour the beaten whites into the dry ingredients and mix with your hands until a sticky dough forms.

Preheat the oven to 300°F and line two baking sheets with parchment paper. Roll the dough into 1-inch balls and place on the baking sheets, spacing them 1 inch apart. Flatten the cookies slightly, then let stand on the baking sheet for 15 minutes.

Bake the cookies until the tops are cracked and the cookies are golden brown, about 20 minutes. Let cool on the baking sheet for 2 to 3 minutes, then transfer to a wire rack and let cool completely. The cookies will keep for up to 3 days in an airtight container.

BABA AU RHUM

MAKES 1 CAKE; SERVES 8

Though this yeasted rum-soaked cake is French in origin, it's popular in Naples, likely introduced there by French chefs, and can also be found at almost every patisserie in Sicily, baked into individual cakes resting in a long tray of rummy syrup. Though the cake is often studded with currants, I add tart dried Blenheim apricots to my version.

⅓ cup dried sulfured Blenheim apricots

1 tablespoon good-quality dark rum

5 tablespoons unsalted butter, at room temperature

½ cup milk

1 package (2¼ teaspoons) active dry yeast

2 tablespoons sugar

2 eggs, at room temperature

1⅔ cups all-purpose flour

½ teaspoon kosher salt

FOR THE RUM SYRUP

2¼ cups water

1½ cups sugar

1 cup good-quality dark rum

¾ teaspoon pure vanilla extract

Softly whipped cream, for serving

Combine the apricots and rum in a small bowl and set aside.

Melt 1 tablespoon of the butter and brush a 5-cup-capacity (6½ by 3½-inch) tube pan or kugelhopf mold with the melted butter, taking care to coat every crevice of the pan.

Heat the milk until it's just warm to the touch, then pour it into the bowl of a stand mixer fitted with the paddle attachment. Stir in the yeast and sugar and let for stand 5 minutes.

With the mixer on low speed, first add the eggs, then the flour, salt, and remaining 4 tablespoons butter. Raise the speed to medium-high and beat for 5 minutes. Scrape down the bowl and beater to form the dough into a ball. It will be very soft. Cover the bowl with a damp towel and let rise in a warm place until doubled in size, about 1 hour.

Drain the apricots and finely chop, fold them into the dough with a spatula, and spoon the dough into the prepared pan. Smooth the top, cover the pan with a damp towel, and let rise in a warm place until the dough reaches the top of the pan, 50 minutes to 1 hour. Meanwhile, preheat the oven to 375°F and set a wire rack over a baking sheet.

Prepare the rum syrup: Place the water and sugar in a small saucepan and cook over high heat until the sugar dissolves. Pour into a measuring cup or bowl and let cool. Stir in the rum and vanilla and set aside.

Bake the cake for 20 to 25 minutes, or until a toothpick inserted into the center of the cake comes out clean. Let cool for 10 minutes, then turn out onto the wire rack. Poke the cake all over with a toothpick (this will allow it to better absorb the syrup), then spoon 2 cups of the rum syrup very slowly onto the warm cake, allowing it all to soak in thoroughly.

To serve the cake, cut it into wedges and transfer to plates. Serve some of the remaining rum syrup spooned around each slice and top with a spoonful of softly whipped cream.

BONÉT

SERVES 8

This is one of the classic home-style desserts of northern Italy and shows up on the menu of most of the small family-run trattorias throughout Piedmont's wine region. It's flanlike in texture, but the small amount of ground amaretti cookies gives it some extra structure, so it is sliceable. I love the contrast of the rich cocoa pudding with the gentle bitterness of the dark caramel that lines the pan, and the amaretti gives the dessert a subtle background note of almond. Because the chocolate flavor derives entirely from cocoa, use the best-quality Dutch-processed cocoa you can find. This dessert can be made up to a day ahead; unmold just before serving. I make this in a slightly larger, 1½-pound, loaf pan.

2 cups (3½ ounces) amaretti, homemade (page 255) or store-bought	¾ cup Dutch-processed cocoa powder, plus more for garnish
4¼ cups whole milk	½ cup coffee liqueur or dark rum
2 eggs plus 4 egg yolks	Softly whipped cream, for serving (optional)
1 cup sugar	Candied orange peel, for serving (optional)
1 teaspoon vanilla extract	

Put the cookies in a food processor and process until finely ground. Set aside.

Pour the milk into a small saucepan and heat over medium heat until warm to the touch. Remove from the heat and set aside.

Preheat the oven to 325°F. In the bowl of a stand mixer fitted with the whisk attachment, beat the eggs, yolks, ½ cup of the sugar, and the vanilla on medium-high speed until the mixture has doubled in volume and is light, frothy, and cloudlike, about 10 minutes. Fold in the ground cookies and cocoa powder, then whisk in the warm milk and coffee liqueur.

In a small saucepan over medium heat, melt the remaining ½ cup sugar. Cook the sugar, swirling the pan occasionally, until the caramel is very dark but not burned. Remove from the heat and immediately pour into a 12¼ by 4½-inch loaf pan, tilting the pan so the caramel coats the bottom completely.

Whisk the batter, then pour it into the prepared pan. Place the pan in a hot water bath and bake until the pudding is set (it should jiggle only slightly in the center), about 1½ hours.

Remove the pan from the water bath. Let cool to room temperature, then transfer to the refrigerator and let cool completely. Before serving, dip the bottom of the pan into a pan of hot water and let stand for 30 seconds. Run a thin knife around the pudding, then unmold onto a platter. Dust with cocoa powder. To serve, cut into eight slices and transfer to plates. Serve with a spoonful of softly whipped cream and some candied orange peel.

ANISE SEED BREAKFAST COOKIES

MAKES 3 DOZEN COOKIES

This is a crispy double-baked cookie, similar to biscotti, perfect for dunking in coffee or wine. It's a bit unusual because it's leavened with yeast, and it emerges from the first trip to the oven looking more like a cake, which you then unmold, slice, and bake a second time until crisp and brown. I put quite a lot of anise into the batter, giving the cookies a strong black licorice flavor and a lot of personality.

---

9 eggs

1½ cups sugar

3 cups plus 2 tablespoons all-purpose flour

1 packet (2¼ teaspoons) instant yeast

1 teaspoon honey

1 heaping tablespoon whole anise seeds

Line a 13 by 9-inch pan with parchment paper. In a stand mixer fitted with the whisk attachment, whip the eggs and sugar on high speed until creamy, pale, and voluminous, 8 minutes. Decrease the mixer speed to low and add the flour, yeast, honey, and anise seeds and mix until combined. Pour the mixture into the pan and let stand at room temperature for 40 minutes. Preheat the oven to 400°F.

Bake for 30 minutes, until puffed and golden and a toothpick inserted into the center comes out clean. Let cool on a rack for 10 minutes, then run a knife around the edges of the pan and turn the cake out onto the cooling rack and let cool completely.

When the cake is cool, trim about ⅓ inch from the ends and sides of the cake (it will be a dark brown color) and discard. Cut the cake crosswise into three equal pieces, then slice each piece crosswise into ⅓-inch-thick slices (you should get about a dozen from each cake third). Arrange the slices in a single layer on baking sheets, transfer to the oven, and bake until golden brown and hard, 20 to 30 minutes. Transfer to a wire rack and let cool completely, then store in an airtight container. The cookies will keep for several weeks.

MELIGA COOKIES

MAKES ABOUT 5 DOZEN COOKIES

I owe my enthusiasm for these cornbread cookies to my wonderful ex-husband, Renato Sardo. When Renato and I lived together in Italy, we ate these almost every day for breakfast. *Meliga* cookies are to Renato as madeleines were to Proust: the comfort food of childhood. *Meliga* is the Piedmontese dialect word for cornmeal. Corn is much easier to grow in the mountainous and cold northern regions of Italy, so this area developed its own version of the sugar cookie with polenta in addition to flour.

Cookies for breakfast is one of the awesome aspects of life in Italy and a custom that should take hold here, especially since they're probably more healthful than most breakfast cereals. Of course, the cookies are equally good as dessert, served alongside espresso or vin santo and maybe some pieces of bittersweet chocolate.

---

1 cup (2 sticks) plus 5 tablespoons unsalted butter, at room temperature

1 cup sugar

2 egg yolks

2 cups all-purpose flour, plus more for dusting

1½ cups polenta

1 teaspoon vanilla extract

Zest of 1 lemon

In a stand mixer fitted with the paddle attachment, beat the butter and sugar on high speed until light and fluffy. Decrease the speed to low, add the egg yolks, and mix just to combine, then add the flour, polenta, vanilla extract, and lemon zest and mix until a dough forms.

Transfer the dough to a sheet of plastic wrap, wrap tightly, and refrigerate for 30 minutes.

Preheat the oven to 375°F and line two baking sheets with parchment paper.

Dust a work surface with flour and roll the dough to a thickness of ¼ inch. Cut the dough into rounds with a 1½-inch round cutter and transfer to the baking sheets. Bake until just golden, 8 to 10 minutes, then transfer to a cooling rack and let cool completely.

HONEY NOUGAT

MAKES ONE 8-INCH PAN; 60 SMALL PIECES

This is a fairly simple candy to make at home that is lovely for holiday gift giving or as a make-ahead dessert for a party. Nougat is traditionally studded with nuts—almonds, hazelnuts, and pistachios, usually, or a mixture of these—which gives a nice roasty flavor and textural contrast to the soft meringue. You could add tart cherries or finely chopped candied lemon or orange peel to the mix, or do what they do in Italy and stir in some whole coffee beans. I've also made a version in which granola is swapped for the nuts—very tasty, though it does not keep as well. Edible wafer paper is essential; nougat is very sticky, and the wafer paper makes cutting and handling it possible.

2 sheets edible wafer paper	¾ cup honey
2½ cups nuts, such as almonds, hazelnuts, pistachios, walnuts, or a mixture	½ cup water
	2 egg whites, at room temperature
2 cups sugar	Pinch of kosher salt

Preheat the oven to 325°F. Lightly grease an 8-inch square baking pan with butter. Line the bottom of the pan with wafer paper, trimming it to fit.

Spread the nuts on a rimmed baking sheet and toast in the oven, stirring once, until just beginning to turn light golden brown in spots, about 10 minutes. Let cool. Coarsely chop and set aside.

Combine the sugar, honey, and water in a heavy saucepan over medium heat. Stir until the sugar dissolves. Increase the heat and boil until the mixture registers 252°F on a candy thermometer.

Meanwhile, beat the egg whites and salt in a stand mixer fitted with a whisk attachment until soft peaks form.

With the mixer running, gradually stream the hot syrup into the egg whites, taking care to avoid the sides of the mixer bowl as much as possible. Increase the speed to high and beat until the meringue is thick (it will first gain volume and then deflate and thicken), 5 minutes. Working quickly, stir in the toasted nuts by hand and mix until well combined.

Transfer the nougat to the baking pan, spreading in an even layer. Top with the second sheet of wafer paper. Using an offset spatula or small rolling pin, press the nougat into a smooth, even layer. Cover the pan with a piece of plastic wrap, then weight down the nougat with a heavy pot or a stack of books. Let stand overnight.

Remove the nougat sheet from the pan and transfer to a work surface; discard the paper. Run a large sharp knife under hot tap water and wipe dry. Cut the nougat lengthwise into six strips, then cut each strip crosswise into ten pieces, occasionally reheating the knife under hot water and wiping dry between cuts. Wrap each piece in a small square of cellophane or wax paper. Nougat will keep in a cool, dark place for several weeks.

RUMTOPF FOR FAKERS

MAKES ONE 32-OUNCE JAR

Rumtopf is a tradition in northern Europe. The concept is simple: ripe fruit at the peak of the season is tossed in a crock with sugar and high-proof spirits and left to decay slowly and deliciously. If left for months, the result is as much a premade rum punch as a fruit dessert. As the fruit slowly breaks down, it becomes infused with the rum and sugar. Back in the day, this was a way to preserve a bit of the taste of summer (and some vitamin C, I presume) for the winter months. I actually prefer a shorter aging time on my *rumtopf* so it's more like a boozy fruit salad. Mine does not usually make it to 3 months old—I prepare it fresh and let it sit for a week or so. At any point in its aging process, *rumtopf* is a great way to dress up ice cream, or it can be made into a quick trifle by layering it with madeleine cookies or ladyfingers and whipped cream and letting everything meld for a couple of hours.

Peel the stone fruit and cut into eighths (peaches and nectarines) or quarters (plums and apricots). Put in a large bowl, add the strawberries, and stir to combine. Measure the fruit and add ½ cup sugar for every cup of fruit, stirring well to coat. Let stand at room temperature for 30 minutes.

Transfer the fruit and any accumulated juices to a large glass jar or crock and add enough rum to cover. Let stand in a cool area of your house for at least a week or up to 3 months. When you're ready to serve, pour the cordial into small glasses and add a few pieces of the boozy fruit to each glass. The fruit and some of the liquid is also good spooned over ice cream or pound cake.

---

3 pounds stone fruit, such as peaches, nectarines, plums, and apricots, or a mixture	Sugar
	Overproof rum
1 pound strawberries, hulled and halved	

LEMON GRANITA

SERVES 6

When I spent time in Sicily, this was actually a staple breakfast food in summertime—scoops of fresh granita piled into a halved hot brioche. The granita melted into the warm bread, forming a syrupy sticky bun that you had to eat fast. That—plus a few espressos—would tide you through until dinnertime on a blazing-hot day.

---

4 lemons

4 cups water

¾ cup sugar

Zest the lemons, reserving the zest, then cut the fruit in half and juice the fruit; you should have ⅔ cup lemon juice.

In a nonreactive pot over medium-high heat, stir together the water and sugar. Bring to a boil, then lower the heat and simmer for 2 minutes, stirring to dissolve the sugar. Add the lemon juice and lemon zest to the sugar syrup. Remove from the heat, cover, and let steep for 30 minutes.

Strain the mixture through a fine-mesh sieve into a 9 by 13-inch nonreactive pan, transfer to the refrigerator, and let cool completely. Once cool, transfer the pan to the freezer and freeze until solid (overnight is best).

Shortly before serving, remove the granita from the freezer and, using the tines of a fork, scrape the granita into fluffy, icy snow. Return to the freezer until ready to serve. Just before serving, use a spoon to scoop the granita into chilled coupes or small bowls and serve immediately.

CARAMELIZED APPLES

SERVES 4

This simple, sweet-savory preparation is a nice dessert for fall or winter. Apples and pork are a natural pairing, so the idea of cooking the fruit in lard rather than butter isn't as novel as it may sound. The lard adds a savory undertone to the caramelized fruit, but make no mistake—this is definitely dessert.

These apples, softened and sticky, with dark caramelized edges, are only enhanced by a scoop of vanilla ice cream or whipped cream.

¼ cup Rendered Pork Fat (Lard) (page 21) or unsalted butter

¼ cup sugar

4 large tart-firm apples (such as Granny Smith), cored and halved

1 teaspoon ground cinnamon

1 teaspoon freshly squeezed lemon juice

Heat the lard in a 10-inch cast-iron frying pan over medium heat. Once melted, sprinkle the sugar into the pan and cook, stirring occasionally, until the sugar begins to caramelize. Cook without stirring until the sugar is a light golden brown, about 3 minutes, watching carefully so the sugar doesn't scorch.

Add the apples cut side down and cook without turning for 10 minutes, until the apples have begun to soften and caramelize. Flip the apples over and continue cooking until the apples are very tender and the liquid in the pan has reduced to a syrupy glaze, 5 to 10 minutes more. Remove from the heat, add the cinnamon and lemon juice, and stir to combine. Serve warm.

BUTTERMILK PANNA COTTA

MAKES 6 PANNA COTTA

Panna cotta is a northern Italian classic. The original version of this was made by reducing cream over a low wood fire (hence the name: cooked [*cotta*] cream [*panna*]), which is truly delicious but a little too time-consuming for today's schedules, so the modern versions are made with gelatin. My panna cotta has equal parts heavy cream and buttermilk, as I like the tangy flavor contributed by the buttermilk. I also love making panna cotta from raw (unpasteurized) cream, which gives it a slightly richer and more complex flavor.

In the recipe below, I suggest using a basic ramekin for the panna cotta and then inverting it to make a little flanlike custard. I have also had great success making this recipe using half-pint jam jars with a bit of fresh fruit or jam spooned into the bottom. When time is not an issue, I also have poured the panna mixture into hollowed-out duck or chicken eggs. It's a beautiful presentation that is fun to eat, especially appropriate for an Easter feast.

1½ teaspoons gelatin	1½ cups buttermilk (page 23)
1 tablespoon water	1 vanilla bean, split and scraped
1½ cups heavy cream	6 tablespoons jam (optional)
½ cup sugar	

In a medium bowl, dissolve the gelatin in the water.

In a saucepan, heat the cream and sugar over medium heat until the sugar has dissolved and begins to bubble on the edges of the pan. Remove from the heat and whisk into the bowl containing the gelatin.

Whisk in the buttermilk and vanilla bean seeds, then strain through a fine-mesh sieve into a bowl.

Spoon a tablespoon of jam into the bottom of each of six 8-ounce ramekins or half-pint canning jars. Divide the panna cotta mixture evenly among the ramekins, then transfer to the refrigerator and refrigerate until cold and set, at least 4 hours or overnight. Serve the custards in their ramekins.

BUTTERMILK PIE

MAKES ONE 9-INCH PIE; SERVES 6 TO 8

I love the sweet, lemony tang of this custard pie, a staple of the American South—often called chess pie—that is made almost entirely with pantry staples. The pie should be served at room temperature or cold, otherwise it will be difficult to slice cleanly; I like to serve slices with fresh berries and cream, or—to amplify its tanginess—a spoonful of lemon curd.

---

3 cups sugar

½ cup (1 stick) unsalted butter, melted

6 eggs

½ cup all-purpose flour

1 tablespoon lemon juice

½ teaspoon lemon zest

1 teaspoon vanilla extract

½ teaspoon kosher salt

¼ teaspoon ground cinnamon

¼ teaspoon ground nutmeg

1½ cups buttermilk (preferably whole milk, page 23)

1 unbaked Buttery Piecrust (page 278)

Preheat the oven to 350°F.

In a large bowl, whisk together the sugar, melted butter, eggs, flour, lemon juice and zest, vanilla, salt, cinnamon, and nutmeg. Whisk in the buttermilk, then pour the filling into the unbaked pie crust and bake until the pie is golden brown on top and the center jiggles slightly, 45 to 50 minutes.

Transfer to a wire rack and let cool completely before slicing.

JAM TARTLETS

MAKES 12 TARTLETS OR ONE 9-INCH TART

This versatile dessert is my go-to when I'm in need of a quick sweet-tooth fix and is one of my most requested recipes. In the winter, I use tart apricot jam that my mother makes using fruit from the Blenheim tree in her backyard; in late summer, slices of peach can be substituted for the jam.

You can make individual tartlets in a muffin tin or bake a large tart using a 9-inch tart pan with a removable bottom. The custard is flexible, too—if you don't have crème fraîche, substitute plain yogurt (Greek-style works especially well) or ricotta. Using "00" flour results in a crust with an especially tender crumb; cake flour yields a similar result. All-purpose flour will work, but the crust will be slightly more cookielike.

FOR THE CRUST	FOR THE FILLING
½ cup (1 stick) unsalted butter, melted	1 cup crème fraîche, Greek yogurt, or ricotta
1¼ cups "00" flour, cake flour, or all-purpose flour	1 egg
½ cup sugar	2 tablespoons sugar or mild honey
½ teaspoon vanilla extract	¼ teaspoon vanilla extract
½ teaspoon almond extract	¼ teaspoon ground nutmeg
¼ teaspoon salt	12 tablespoons apricot jam

Preheat the oven to 350°F.

Make the crust: In a medium bowl combine the melted butter, flour, sugar, vanilla, almond extract, and salt. Mix with a spoon until it comes together into a crumbly dough.

Divide the dough evenly among the cups in the muffin tin and, using your fingertips, loosely press the dough into the pan. Don't worry about making it perfect; it will meld together as it bakes (alternatively, if you are making one tart, press the dough into a 9-inch removable-bottom tart pan). Transfer to the oven and bake until light golden brown, 10 minutes.

Make the filling: In a bowl, whisk together the crème fraîche, egg, sugar, vanilla, and nutmeg. Pour the mixture into the parbaked crusts, dividing evenly among the cups. Top each with 1 tablespoon of the apricot jam (if using a muffin tin) or spread the jam evenly over the top (if making one large tart).

Return the pan to the oven and bake until the custard puffs and is golden brown and the jam is beginning to caramelize, about 45 minutes more. Remove from the oven and let cool for 15 minutes, then use an offset spatula to transfer the tartlets to a wire rack and let cool completely.

WALNUT TART

MAKES ONE 9-INCH TART; SERVES 6 TO 8

This tart is halfway between a big sticky cookie and a pie. It's similar to pecan pie in spirit but less cloying. This tart is quick to assemble, difficult to mess up, and keeps well at room temperature—you can make it in the morning and serve it for that evening's dessert. Serve it solo or with whipped cream.

1 unbaked Buttery Piecrust (page 278)

6 tablespoons unsalted butter

½ cup packed light brown sugar

¼ cup honey

2 teaspoons pure vanilla extract

Zest of 1 lemon

¼ teaspoon kosher salt

2 eggs

2 cups (½ pound) walnut halves

Roll the dough on a lightly floured surface with a lightly floured rolling pin into a 12-inch round. Fit the dough into a 9-inch removable-bottom tart pan and trim the excess dough. Lightly prick the bottom all over with a fork. Chill until firm, at least 30 minutes.

Preheat the oven to 350°F and put a rimmed baking sheet on the center rack.

Melt the butter in a small heavy saucepan over medium heat. Add the brown sugar, whisking until smooth. Remove from the heat and whisk in the honey, vanilla, lemon zest, and salt.

Lightly beat the eggs in a medium bowl, then whisk the honey mixture into the eggs.

Arrange the walnuts in a single layer in the tart shell and pour the honey mixture evenly over them. Place the tart pan on the hot baking sheet and bake until filling is set and the crust is brown, 50 minutes to 1 hour. Cool completely, then slice into wedges and serve.

BUTTERY PIECRUST

MAKES TWO 9-INCH CRUSTS

This recipe dates back to my brief days as a professional baker and was inspired by the crusts on my grandmother's apple pie, which were golden and flaky and are partially responsible for my love of cooking. It's a very short crust, with a decent amount of fat in proportion to the flour, and though it can be a bit tricky to work with, you'll be rewarded with a very fine pastry. Don't be discouraged if the dough at first looks crumbly; when you wrap the dough you can gather up any lose crumbles with the plastic wrap, forming it into a cohesive ball.

2½ cups all-purpose flour

1 tablespoon sugar

1 teaspoon kosher salt

1 cup (2 sticks) unsalted butter, very cold, cut into ¼-inch cubes

6 tablespoons ice-cold water

In the bowl of a food processor, combine the flour, sugar, and salt and pulse once or twice to mix. Add the cold cubed butter to the processor and pulse three or four times, until the butter is in pea-size pieces. Drizzle the water over the flour mixture and pulse a few times, just until the dough comes together in a shaggy ball.

Divide the dough into two and wrap each half tightly in plastic wrap, using the plastic wrap to help gather up any loose crumbles of dough. Press each ball into a disk, transfer to the refrigerator, and refrigerate for 30 minutes before rolling (if you refrigerate it longer, let the dough stand at room temperature for 10 minutes before rolling). The dough will keep, refrigerated, for up to 3 days or it can be tightly wrapped and frozen for up to 3 months. Thaw overnight in the refrigerator before using.

On a lightly floured work surface, with a lightly floured rolling pin, roll the dough into a thin, even circle about 12 inches in diameter, beginning in the center and working outward.

SAVORY-SWEET RICOTTA CHEESECAKE

MAKES ONE 8-INCH CAKE; SERVES 6

When I worked as a cheese maker for a year in Italy, I spent about 3 months on a farm in Tuscany with a few hundred sheep. We started making cheese first thing in the morning when the sheep's milk was still warm. By 10 a.m., all the cheese was on a draining board, and we made ricotta from the remaining whey. We added a bit of the previous day's whey to increase the acidity and speed coagulation and tossed in a skinned fig branch from the tree in the courtyard (green fig branches are a natural source of vegetable rennet and help the cheese firm up).

Within an hour of bringing the whey to a boil, we were scooping off huge hot ladlefuls of the ricotta for lunch, which we would dress with good olive oil and salt. A day later, any surplus ricotta would be used to fill pastas and to make simple cheesecakes. The extra day of drying was important, ensuring that the ricotta was crumbly and not wet, which in turn yielded a fluffier, lighter cake or filling.

This recipe is inspired by memories of that ricotta. It's a simple disk of baked cheese, gently sweetened and set with eggs, with a more pronounced milky flavor and crumblier texture than traditional cheesecake (most of which is made with cream cheese). Because American ricotta is not usually basket-drained and tends to have higher moisture than what you find in Italy, I also add a bit of cornstarch, which will help the cake set. I like to fold fresh berries, like blackberries or raspberries, into this before baking or scatter berries over the baked cake. It's also good with a spoonful of jam on top.

Preheat the oven to 350°F. Brush an 8-inch cast-iron frying pan with the olive oil and set aside.

In the bowl of a stand mixer fitted with the paddle attachment, add the ricotta, granulated sugar, cornstarch, and nutmeg. Beat on medium speed until smooth, then add the egg and egg yolks and mix on low speed until just combined.

Transfer the ricotta mixture to the prepared pan and bake until golden brown and puffed on top and beginning to pull away from the sides of the pan, 30 to 35 minutes.

Transfer to a wire rack and let cool completely. To serve, invert the cake onto a cutting board and dust with confectioners' sugar. Cut into wedges and transfer to plates, scattered with fresh berries.

---

2 teaspoons extra-virgin olive oil

2 cups ricotta, homemade, (page 52) or store-bought

¼ cup granulated sugar

1 tablespoon cornstarch

Pinch of nutmeg

1 egg plus 2 egg yolks

Confectioners' sugar, for dusting (optional)

Berries or jam, for serving (optional)

OLD-SCHOOL POUND CAKE (WITH LARD)

MAKES ONE CAKE; SERVES 8 TO 10

Lard was once America's primary baking fat. Butter was relatively more expensive until the dairy industry centralized and consolidated in the 1920s, when butter became cheaper than pig fat. With the advent of technology in the 1950s that gave us solidified vegetable oils, both butter and lard went into a period of disfavor that they are only now beginning to recover from. In short: There were lots of big agro-industrial forces at play that lead to lard's fall from grace, things that had very little to do with its healthfulness or its superlative baking qualities.

Use best-quality lard for this cake, as it contains a good amount of it with relatively few other ingredients to obstruct its flavor. Your lard should be sweet and fresh, with no smell of pork or of rancidity. If you are making the lard yourself, use leaf lard to render (see page 21). This cake is exceptionally moist, with a fine crumb. It's good on its own or topped with sliced fresh fruit and whipped cream.

1 cup Rendered Pork Fat (Lard) (page 21) or unsalted butter, at room temperature

3 cups sugar

5 eggs

3 cups all-purpose flour

½ teaspoon salt

½ teaspoon baking powder

1 cup whole milk

1 teaspoon vanilla extract

Preheat the oven to 350°F. Grease a Bundt or tube pan or a 1½-pound-capacity loaf pan with lard, dust with flour, and set aside.

Using a stand mixer fitted with the paddle attachment, beat the lard on high until soft and creamy, about 2 minutes. Reduce the speed to medium and gradually add the sugar. Add the eggs one at a time, beating after each addition.

Combine the flour, salt, and baking powder in a bowl. With the mixer on low, add the dry ingredients to the mixer, alternating with the milk, beginning and ending with the flour. Add the vanilla and mix to combine.

Transfer the batter to the prepared pan and bake for 1 to 1½ hours, until a toothpick inserted into the center of the cake comes out clean.

Let cool on a wire rack for 10 minutes, then turn out of the pan and let cool completely on the wire rack. The cake will keep, well wrapped and refrigerated, for several days; let it come to room temperature before serving.

GINGERBREAD

MAKES ONE 9-INCH CAKE; SERVES 8 TO 10

This is grown-up gingerbread, dark and spicy, made with both fresh and powdered ginger and a small amount of cocoa powder, which gives it an almost black color. I first developed this recipe when I was working on a dude ranch in Montana as a baker—it was a favorite with the cowboys and the guests and has remained in rotation ever since. Serve wedges with cream or ice cream or simply dusted with confectioners' sugar, sometimes I'll add candied citrus peel, as shown here. If you prefer, this cake can also be baked in a large (1½-pound-capacity) loaf pan.

½ cup (1 stick) unsalted butter, cut into cubes

1 cup molasses (not blackstrap)

¾ cup sugar

1 cup boiling water

1 egg

2 tablespoons grated fresh ginger

2½ cups all-purpose flour

½ cup cocoa powder

1½ teaspoons baking soda

1 teaspoon ground ginger

1 teaspoon ground cinnamon

½ teaspoon ground nutmeg

½ teaspoon kosher salt

Preheat the oven to 350°F. Grease a 9-inch round cake pan and line with parchment paper.

In a large bowl, add the butter, molasses, and sugar. Pour in the boiling water and whisk to combine, then whisk in the egg and fresh ginger.

In a medium bowl, combine the flour, cocoa, baking soda, ground ginger, cinnamon, nutmeg, and salt. Stir the dry ingredients into the wet ingredients until completely incorporated, then transfer to the prepared baking pan.

Bake until the gingerbread springs back when touched and a toothpick inserted into the center comes out clean, 35 to 40 minutes (if the top begins to brown too much before the cake is cooked through, cover the pan with aluminum foil).

Let cool on a wire rack for 10 minutes, then turn out of the pan, peel off the parchment paper, and turn the gingerbread right side up. Let cool completely, then cut into wedges and serve.

ALMOND TORTA

MAKES ONE 9-INCH CAKE; SERVES 8 TO 10

This is a sophisticated cake—dense, and gently sweet. I often serve it with a fruit compote and a big spoonful of crème fraîche, then dunk any leftovers into my coffee the next morning. This is my version of the hazelnut cake that I grew to love in northern Italy, where it is a standard dessert option in all of the simple trattorias. In Piedmont, they use a special local variety of hazelnut for this cake.

If you want to bump up the nutty flavor, try roasting whole almonds or hazelnuts, rubbing their skins off and letting them cool, then grinding the roasted nuts into flour in a food processor. Roasted nuts are almost universally more complex in flavor, but commercially available nut flour is rarely made from roasted nuts, as it goes rancid more quickly.

If you want to make a gluten-free version, replace the all-purpose flour with the same amount of additional nut flour. The resulting cake will be slightly denser but no less delicious. When you're mixing the batter it will seem too thick, but trust me: the cake will turn out light and moist.

½ cup (1 stick) unsalted butter

4 eggs, separated

1 cup sugar

½ teaspoon kosher salt

½ teaspoon vanilla extract

½ teaspoon almond extract (if using hazelnut flour, omit this ingredient)

Zest of 1 lemon

2½ cups almond or hazelnut flour

½ cup all-purpose flour

Preheat the oven to 325°F. Lightly grease a 9-inch round cake pan and line with parchment paper.

In a small saucepan over medium heat, melt the butter. In the bowl of a stand mixer fitted with the paddle attachment, beat the egg yolks, sugar, and salt on medium speed until light and pale yellow, about 4 minutes. Reduce the mixer speed to low, then stream in the melted butter and continue mixing until combined. Stir in the vanilla extract, almond extract, and lemon zest.

In a small bowl, combine the nut flour and all-purpose flour. With the mixer on low, add the flours to the egg mixture, mixing until just combined.

Beat the egg whites until they hold soft peaks. Stir one-third of the beaten whites into the nut flour mixture to lighten it—the batter will be quite thick at this point. Fold in the remaining beaten whites in two additions, mixing until no white streaks remain.

Transfer the batter to the prepared pan and smooth the top with an offset spatula. Bake until the cake is golden brown and pulling away from the sides of the pan and a toothpick inserted into the center of the cake comes out clean, 30 to 35 minutes.

Let cool in the pan for 10 minutes, then turn out onto a wire rack and let cool completely. Cut into wedges and serve with a spoonful of crème fraîche and some sliced fruit or fruit compote.

APPLE TORTA

MAKES ONE 9-INCH CAKE; SERVES 8

This cake can be sliced thin and dressed up with whipped cream or crème fraîche for an elegant dessert or scooped onto plates straight from the pan with a spoon and topped with vanilla ice cream for a rustic crowd-pleaser. The cake stays very moist because of the apple chunks, which cook into soft pockets of applesauce when the cake is baked. I have also experimented with making this cake with lard instead of butter with excellent results (apples and lard are soul mates).

---

10 large sweet-tart apples, peeled, cored, and diced

½ cup water

1 cup (2 sticks) unsalted butter

2 cups sugar

2 eggs

3 cups all-purpose flour

1 tablespoon ground nutmeg

2 teaspoons baking soda

1 teaspoon ground allspice

½ teaspoon ground cinnamon

Softly whipped crème fraîche or cream, for serving

Preheat the oven to 350°F. Grease a 9-inch cake pan or cast-iron frying pan; if using a cake pan, line the bottom with a piece of parchment and grease the parchment.

In a large saucepan over medium heat, combine the diced apples and water and cook, stirring, until the apples have begun to soften, about 10 minutes. Remove from the heat and let cool.

In the bowl of a stand mixer fitted with the paddle attachment, cream the butter and sugar on high speed until light and fluffy, about 5 minutes. Reduce the speed to low and add the eggs one at a time, mixing after each addition.

In a medium bowl, sift together the flour, nutmeg, baking soda, allspice, and cinnamon. With the mixer on low, gradually add the dry ingredients until well combined. Fold in the apples and any accumulated juice.

Transfer the batter to the prepared pan and bake until the cake is golden on top and pulling away from the sides of the pan and a toothpick inserted into the center comes out clean, 50 minutes to 1 hour.

Transfer to a wire rack and let cool completely. Cut into wedges and serve with softly whipped crème fraîche or cream.

Acknowledgments

I would like to thank the following people for their help and guidance in developing *Home Cooked*: Jessica Battilana, Jenny Wapner, Leslie Jonath, Brown Cannon, Gina Sabatella, Betsy Stromberg, and Clara Sankey.

This project would not have been possible without the creative support, mentorship and sounding board provided by my colleagues from Belcampo: Todd Robinson, Matthew Runeare, Nate Morr, Talia Dillman, Bronwen Hanna-Korpi, Laura Beaudrow, and Rachel Graville.

As a mom trying to look like I have it all together, I need to call out the women who actually made me look good, took care of my kid, and gave me pats on the back during the process of writing and shooting this book: Elena Gania, Bianca Pardini, Shawn Burke, Mindy Mitchell, and Mindy Berla.

Index

Photographs on pages ii, 115 (right), 173, 236 (left), and 240 by Erin Kunkel.

Library of Congress Cataloging-in-Publication Data
Fernald, Anya, author.
  Home cooked : essential recipes for a new way to cook / by Anya Fernald with
Jessica Battilana.
    pages cm
  Includes bibliographical references and index.
1. Cooking. I. Battilana, Jessica, author. II. Title.
  TX714.F467 2016
  641.5—dc23
                             2015033515

Hardcover ISBN: 978-1-60774-840-3
eBook ISBN: 978-1-60774-841-0

Printed in China

Interior design by Betsy Stromberg

Cover design by Robert van Horne

10 9 8 7 6 5 4 3 2 1

First Edition